DIRECTLY HOME

REFRESHINGLY SIMPLE STEPS TO
PROFOUND PEACE

DIRECTLY
HOME

BARRETT SELF

ISBN: 9798778341098

Edited by Adrien Palmer (apwordandsound.com)
Book cover design by Amier (wildeaglestudio.com)

Published by Exhale Now Co
exhalenow.co

First Edition

DEDICATED TO

Each person who reached out and shared their heart
through email, private message, video call or in-person
session over the last few years. Our conversations have
shaped and crafted the expression in these pages. This book
would not be possible without you.

DIRECTLY HOME

CONTENTS

DIRECTLY HOME

ACKNOWLEDGMENTS

Special thanks to my editor, Adrien Palmer, for fielding all the endless re-drafts and late-night calls throughout the writing process. Thanks to my long-time friend and colleague Will Weatherly for all the insights, inspiration and friendship. Thanks to both my parents for their love and support and to my dog Bailey for secretly writing this book and letting me take the credit.

DIRECTLY HOME

HOME

Once, a king fell asleep and dreamed he was a beggar. In his dreaming, he walked like a beggar, talked like a beggar and began to think and feel like a beggar until he forgot he was king at all.

Late in the night, a man who remembered appeared, stirred the king from his bed and led him to the hillside.

'All this is yours,' said the man, pointing across the horizon.

'Surely not,' replied the king. 'I am just a beggar.'

'Most men are beggars,' replied the man. 'Though they do not know it. Go and find that truth that sets them free.'

So the king ventured the hillside until he arrived at a mansion. Inside, he found a rich man counting coins.

'Is this what's true?' Asked the king.

'Yes,' replied the rich man, stacking money. 'Money is the greatest truth. It can buy you all the others.'

Just then a strong gust blew in and scattered the coins into the open field. The rich man fell to his knees, suddenly a beggar, too.

And the king thought surely there was more; *'The truth should not be so easily thrown to the wind.'*

So the king descended the hill until the fields gave way to cobblestone. He took to the path and soon came upon a golden library wrapped in rose bushes. From an upper window, he heard a faint murmur. Grabbing a nearby ladder, he climbed to the third story where inside, he saw piles of books as large as cinder blocks and a learned man with three in each hand.

'Is this what's true?' Asked the king, popping his head through an open window.

'Yes,' replied the learned man, his nose buried in books. 'Knowledge is the highest truth. It can teach you all the others.'

The king reached for one of the smaller, abandoned books. But at the sight of the king's soiled hands, the learned man snatched the book and slammed the window shut, sending the King toppling back to earth.

And the king thought surely there was more; *'The truth should not be so removed from life.'*

So he wandered beside the bed of roses back into the cobbled streets where the gonging of cathedrals filled the air. He followed the sound through gaping gates and once within, discovered a man of belief addressing a congregation.

'Is this what's true?' Interrupted the king.

'Yes!' Replied the believing man. 'Our religion is the only truth. It saves you from all the others.'

The king nodded and slipped into an empty pew as the believing man invited others to believe. But the king did not feel any welling up inside him. He looked to the congregation. Their legs were restless to return to busy lives and their faces, too, were lukewarm with belief.

And the king thought surely there was more; *'The truth should not be so easily doubted.'*

So he journeyed back through the alleys, down the cobblestones, into the fields, across the hill and returned to the man who remembered.

'I went to the rich, but their truth was shaky. I went to the learned, but their truth was lifeless. I went to the religious, but their truth was doubted.'

'You have seen rightly,' said the man. 'But you have gone to the wrong places.'

'And where should I have gone?' Asked the king.

The man closed his eyes.

'Home.'

DIRECTLY HOME

'How much more time will you spend at the wayside inn?
Don't you want to go home?'

Anandamayi Ma

DIRECTLY HOME

1 A PERSONAL JOURNEY HOME

There's a beautiful quote by Kurt Vonnegut in his novel *Slaughterhouse-Five*. It's written very tongue-in-cheek, very jokingly. It's what his main character, war veteran and PTSD sufferer, Billy Pilgrim thinks should be his epitaph; 'Everything was beautiful and nothing hurt.'

For being so little, the phrase carries so much. To me, it captures a very human longing; the longing for enlightenment, God, heaven, paradise, nirvana—or simply peace, happiness, *home*. It's a noble longing. But it doesn't take a lifetime on the streets or time in the trenches to see the joke—everything isn't beautiful.

I grew up in a Christian home. It was filled with good people, Legos and love. For a while, all I saw was beauty. I didn't have to worry about who I'd wake up to in the morning or if dinner would be warm that night and I couldn't fathom tomorrow could hold greater horrors than too much affection. I would be told later in life that I had an innocence that made this possible. I'm not sure that's true. It just took me a while to make up my mind about this place. It takes a mind opened wide to really take in existence. To me, we're too quick to shut it and too encouraged to throw away the key. I kept mine open; innocent until proven guilty. Still, it doesn't take long for the evidence to start pouring in.

I spent most Sundays in children's church observing from the corner. I found it was the best way to be yourself. When you're alone, people aren't trying to put their eyes into you, you have space to see what's true. And if what's true can be seen, surely it appears within the walls built to worship it— and surely having the truth would make things at least a little more beautiful.

But those who were the most certain of truth were often the most judgmental; those who had the most belief often had the least godliness. I remember my childhood pastor's leaked struggle with pornography and eventual divorce. In my late teens, I remember asking my parents why a preacher we'd grown close to at a nearby church was absent and the response including 'jail time' and 'children' and I grew up hearing whispers of a previous pastor's public affair with a choir member. None of this ever made sense to me. I could never reconcile how most people have two people living in them and how their hands often belong to one and their lips the other. What I did sense was that 'God' alone didn't make people beautiful. And having God didn't make the beautiful people not hurt.

I remember my youth leader—a man greater than many, one of love, compassion, humor and presence—bringing a child with a disability into the world. I remember my mother's first marriage and the loss of a child and my extended family members struggle with alcohol and self-love. I remember my dad's best friend dying of cancer at too young an age and I remember a train accident that left my father and uncle without a brother and their parents without a son.

It doesn't matter where we go or what we believe; all people know something not beautiful and something that hurts. The clerk at the DMV, the delivery driver, our pastor and local politician. We've all got our ugly. But it's the ugliest parts of life that are building all the beauty. Winter gives way to spring and shit gives way to orchids and every living thing comes out of every dying thing. We've known this since grade school. But it takes a while longer to see the same truth applies to people. It's often the world's most beautiful people who've been hurt the deepest. In many ways, that's what it takes; the ugly hitting us hard enough for the beauty to fall out.

. . . .

Novelist Samuel Beckett once said of his youth, 'I had little talent for happiness.' And I hear that.

I always had a sadness about me. It wasn't always in the forefront. Sometimes it laid in the background, hiding behind corners and in winter coats. And it could sneak out gradually or all at once. It could slowly creak across floorboards over Sunday mornings or rush in like black clouds over an April sun. No matter how often it happens, you never really settle into the latter; light being everywhere, summer feeling near—then instantly absent.

I spent most of my teens and 20's in the absence— depressed and irritable, angry and reactive. Dissatisfied with myself and dissatisfied with others. I'd faced no great tragedies. I was blessed in that way. But often, whether you've been stalked by trauma or not, it's living in your neighborhood. It's tough to venture past the driveway and not come home without a little on you.

Of course, we don't often see it this way. It's easy to view our lives as having their own arcs, distinct and separate. But no plot is without relationship. We're all living with those who have suffered deeply—even if we haven't. They're in our towns and on our blocks and in our phones. And the scenes from their stories get lines in our book. When we're sad, it's not just our sadness—it's a dash of theirs. It's the added weight of our families, our loved ones. When we're angry, it's not just our anger—it's the reflection of our community's, our culture's. What we're thinking and feeling is a thousand generations in the making. Some people just tune into it more than others. And some grow fond of the sound. That's part of my story.

I was empty, but didn't want to be filled. I was lonely, but couldn't stomach others. In my early 20's, I went to bed every night with my arms full of pillows and my heart dreaming of love, the kind where two broken people who pretended not to want each other somehow fell into orbit and made one whole person possible. I fell in love with that longing. I could write the book on it. I tried to.

I became a musician so I could write sad songs. I found the more down I was, the more beautifully I wrote. So I sought out sadness. I wasn't conscious of it, but it seemed to have a gravity of its own. I listened to sad music, read sad books, formed sad relationships. Soon, it gave me purpose. So I kept ringing the bell and sadness kept showing up. I put it in my ears, in front of my eyes and into my mouth. And beautiful songs came out.

I spent my youth there—creating a home for depression, digging and widening the trenches, raising and thickening the walls, crawling in and calling everything inside, 'me'.

. . . .

In the spring of 2014, I went for a walk. I lived with a friend at the time and our neighborhood wasn't so imaginative—all ready-made townhouses—but there was a beautiful park six blocks and a left turn away. This was fine by me. I had just gotten out of a failed relationship and it always felt right to enter nature in times of transition. It gives room to breathe and reminds us it's natural to change. So far I hadn't changed much. At least not in ways worth noticing. After high school, I'd started college, transferred to another college, joined a band and dropped out of college and worked as a stagehand for a year. In the last six months, I'd moved to a new city, quit an old job, started a new one, ended a relationship and returned back home. These were all great life changes, great worldly changes. But I was still seeing it from the same thought-world, from the same perspectives and worldviews. And I was still the same me.

I remember trouncing through the gravel parking lot and walking down a nearby trail. The flowers and sun were out but it wasn't warm enough to call spring. Regardless of the season, something different was in the air. I don't remember exactly what it was. I don't remember what was happening in my head or my last text message or what I had eaten for breakfast. I just remember an inescapable sense of sadness found me. Not a sadness about anything. It wasn't for the old relationship or an old trauma or a new fear or problem. It was a choiceless sadness; a sadness without cause. It carried a great weight and a great despair that seemed to fill and empty me all at once. My feet stopped walking and the wind died down. And on a familiar path, a deeper awareness stirred.

I was tired of hurting. Tired in the best way possible—the kind of tired and hurting that takes your knees out from under you. I didn't want this anymore. I didn't want this *me* anymore. This *me* with these thoughts and these feelings and these beliefs and perspectives. I didn't want this baseline. I didn't know if I could change. I didn't know if I could look out into the world from a different one. I didn't know what was possible or what could be found, where I'd have to go or who I'd have to meet. But I decided to do the only thing that made sense; whatever was necessary.

. . . .

'Whatever is necessary.' We have this answer for different things; for our bank accounts, our relationships, our achievements; for our responsibilities, our ideals and beliefs. But we often lack it for our own peace. We lack it in the pursuit of real happiness. But for true well-being, it takes that. It takes commitment to not turn *away from*, but rather *into* despair; to not close down, but open up to trauma; to not swim *out of*, but wade *into* the pain and the lack and the boredom and gaze into the chasm that sent them forth.

'Whatever is necessary'—it takes that for real change. Not worldly change or lifestyle change, but *inner* change. Change that happens in the heart and soul.

AN INVITATION

Everyone's selling a romantic healing story, a romantic 'awakening'. I'd love to write one. But the more I try, the more false it sounds. 'Waking up' and self-healing is not a Hollywood thriller. The story doesn't end with us slaying a dragon or escaping from shifting sands. The credits don't roll while we're sitting beneath bodhi trees and denying the devil or riding over palm leaves to the cheers of our biggest fans. The real healing is ordinary—it's you being yourself. It's you finding your original face and giving yourself permission to be what's there. It's the recognition that we do not need the love of others to know love amongst others. We do not need the acceptance, the welcoming of the world to be at one with the world. That's healing; the insides vibing with the outsides. It's the kind of healing that wakes us up out of our collective dramas and divisions. And the more we wake up the more new and miraculous life becomes. Religious thinkers go around asking, 'Why don't miracles happen anymore? Were they true?' To me, they would be better served observing a child; if your heart and mind are new, isn't everything a miracle? The deeper this is felt into, the less concerned we become over belief in miracles. The more we see, by God, we are the miracle. Walking on water, turning it to wine, these are just showmanship. Showmanship draws you in, it grabs your attention. Once attention is grabbed, the teacher lets you in on the secret: ordinary life is the miracle. Breathing is a miracle, walking is a miracle, the body is a miracle—or put religiously, 'The Kingdom of God is *here*.'

But being today's brand of Christian doesn't show it to you. Being today's brand of Buddhist doesn't either. I once believed in Christianity. I once practiced Buddhism. Misery followed me down both paths. If we are a happy person, we can be happy in either. But if we are a miserable person, we will be a miserable Christian or a miserable Buddhist, a miserable Hindu or a miserable atheist. If we are an angry person, we will be an angry rich man or an angry poor man. If we are a lost person we will be a lost wanderer or a lost leader of men. In all cases, we keep getting what we are.

. . . .

The only way to build something new is to get to the foundation. If the house we're living in keeps falling over, we don't buy a new coat of paint or add on a new bedroom. We address the foundation. We dig down to the truth of it. Only by getting to the truth—to the foundation—do we have a chance of security, stability and peace.

This small book is an invitation to your foundation. This foundation isn't reserved for spiritual elitists or religious in-crowds. Enlightenment, awakening and other gilded words aren't for one walk of life and not for another. They are free and available. They are like the wind and the trees and the mountain sky. They are for all people in all places at all times. They are the very nature of life itself. Yes, *this* life, even with all the sorrow and despair. *This* life, even with all the empty stomachs and firing squads and tumors and injustices. *This* life, where so much is unbeautiful and so much hurts.

It's natural to feel this is a fairy tale. After all, we each have piles of anxieties and valleys of depressions. The human family is riddled with weeds of sorrow and oceans of lack and other speechless horrors that only death seems to part from us. On a relative level, this is true; we've all got our troubles—even writers of books like this one. But that which exists in these states isn't the original foundation. It's the rooms above it. It's the hallways and corridors the world has put there. The truth is, regardless of how anxious, depressed, angry or sorrowful we may feel, there was a time when we were not. Not a time where we caught a glimpse of happiness or peace, but a season of life, the very *first* season. That season seems to have passed. It only seems this way because our foundation has slipped out of our awareness— the original 'us' has slipped out of our awareness. That 'us' is the changeless us. It is the inner *light of life*. It is our universalhood. It isn't the physical, but the spiritual. It isn't the mind and body, but the very *source* of life.

. . . .

The following chapter explores this *source*. It's followed by three paths that each lead me back there. Each 'path' is meant for recognizing and returning the mind to that which is changeless. Exploring them serves two purposes. First, the exploration begins guiding us to the deeper truth of ourselves. And second, it starts preparing the conditions so we might live from it. First, we light the match; second, we scatter the shadows. A single-pointedness on any path is all that is needed. Each chapter can stand alone. Each chapter is a small book unto itself. But the exploration of each serves to further the light in all directions.

Within each chapter, the same truth appears. This truth is universal. It is not the property of one religion and not another. It does not belong to the East but not the West. It is beyond comparisons. It is the hidden jewel upon which religion was founded and the means through which life itself comes into being. I have benefited greatly from different expressions of it. These expressions are scattered throughout this book. From my experience, when it comes to truth, little needs saying, but much can use repeating. So I am repeating what I long missed. I am pointing at what I continue to need reminding of again and again. It's my hope that by painting the truth in different shades and textures, that it becomes available in new and vibrant ways.

· · · ·

I feel I would be remiss to not express the following: if you are wrestling with clinical depression or have recently experienced a great loss, open yourself to this book. But I also implore you to find a therapist, life coach or other wellness professional—particularly if you have no experience with meditation. There are many passages in this book that can help steer any open heart towards the *light of life*. There are many excerpts and insights that can serve to draw all of us back Self-wards. But I would not read expecting the words in this book or the practice of them to turn your life around overnight. Invest in someone ready to help.

Lastly, if you are serious about taking this path—seasoned meditators included—I still recommend investing in a therapist, life coach or mentor. They can serve as a helpful mirror, reflecting back to us the barriers and traumas that lay hidden from our vision. Working with someone in this capacity will allow us to shed the past much quicker and step more fully into a new life for ourselves and others.

With that said, I invite you to release the world for a few pages. I invite you to read without your old thoughts; to take on a beginner's mind, the kind that Christ speaks of when he says, 'The Kingdom of God is for children.' He simply says 'children'—he does not mention age.

So I invite you to read like a child, to pour out the stagnant waters that have soured your mind and make room for something living.

Perhaps you're simply looking for meditation tips. Perfect. Create some space—you'll find the ones you need. Perhaps you want to be more centered, more at ease. Beautiful. Remain available, even an intellectual understanding of this book can help with that. Perhaps you want to wake up out of the old 'you', to see from someone new, to discover the place where 'everything is beautiful and nothing hurts.' The more you empty your hands, the more of it you can carry. The more you empty your hands, the greater the possibility for peace, contentedness and acceptance to start entering most-all life experiences. I say 'most-all' because we never know what the next moment will bring. Even the greatest teachers—myself, not amongst them, but included—are not always living and breathing from perfect peace. We are not always the shining beacons of the truths to which we're pointing. But it is only in our distancing from the truths held in pages such as these that we stumble.

Is all of this unlikely to be true? Perhaps. Do you sit at long odds of realizing it? If you want to live your life by the numbers, sure. If little Bobby comes knocking on your door claiming Mrs. Havlecheck is saddling up an ostrich, it's good to have doubts—but it's also good to go look.

I pray you empty your heart and mind and do so.

DIRECTLY HOME

2 PREPARING THE WAY

On a certain day, Jesus was out in the fields of Galilee. Around him, a great crowd had gathered. The crowd grew so large he could no longer pass. 'Jesus, show us a miracle!' They all shouted. Not wanting to disappoint, Jesus called for a glass of water. Now, he'd already turned one glass into wine earlier that day and it was received quite well. He figured he'd double down. As the glass made its way to him, he turned to his disciples, 'Watch! I'll turn this into wine, too!' Jesus called out the magic words and instantly the water turned red. The crowd erupted! They loved it. Jesus turned back to his disciples and winked, 'That's two in one day, boys.' The disciples yawned, 'What else you got?'

. . . .

The actual story of Jesus turning water to wine is a great miracle. It is undeniable. Who can do such a thing? But if we replaced the whole gospel story with it, we'd all grow tired. We'd start asking, 'What else you got?'

If we're overly familiar with any magic trick, it loses its charm—but that doesn't mean it stops being magic. The magic remains. Thought has just organized the wonder.

That's what the disciple's minds have done. And that's what the unconscious mind does with life; 'I know this food, this job, this lover, this trick—yawn. I need something new!' Thus, the purer a mind, the more extraordinary the experience.

Everyone in our lives is a testament to this; our mother, father, sister, brother, mentor, doctor, accountant and cashier. All of them were once enthralled with the magic of life; not thinking of what tomorrow might bring or knowing where the edges of the world lie or what occupies the space between us and there. Once, we were all quietly in tune with the pulse of life. A silent lake—peaceful, serene—happily reflecting the moon and stars. In this original harmony, God was not a distant happening nor was the universe an outside event. Each moment of our lives they were expressing themselves through us.

In this knowing, we had nothing to cling to or run from, bow beneath or stand against. We had nothing to assert, no story to project, no other moments to idolize and nobody to become. We simply were. And because we were and we *only* were, life retained the original magic. In simply the thoughtless knowing, 'I am' life was miraculous.

It's easy to feel that children have an innocence we can't recover; an openness, an exuberance we can't buy back. But a child isn't blissful because she doesn't know what you know. She is blissful because she knows her Self. She is blissful because she is a window for pure consciousness. An adult is the same consciousness suffering its gathering of dust. The dust of opinions, beliefs, stories and preferences. The dust of tomorrow, yesterday, what isn't and what could be.

We can spend a lifetime changing the content of our lives— where we live, how we afford it, who we take with us and what we believe it all means.

Or we can simply embark on the inner journey of touching that original consciousness and through this meeting, rediscover the miracle within.

THE CHANGELESS 'I'

Once, a young girl was troubled. Crying hysterically, she ran to her mother.

'What is *that*?' The girl shrieked, pointing at her shadow.

'Why, that's you!' said the mother.

'That's... me!' exclaimed the girl.

The next day at school, she had to spread the news.

She ran to her friends and pointed to her shadow, 'That's me!'

That afternoon, she had to tell her dad, too; 'That's me!'

Everywhere she went—the grocery store, the park, the dinner table, her grandparent's—the girl kept pointing to her shadow and reminding the world, 'That's me! That's me! That's me!'

After a few weeks, her mother decided she needed to step in. So one evening, she kept the young girl up past bedtime and, once it was dark, escorted the girl to the street corner, beneath the glow of yellow lights. Looking down, the girl suddenly saw her shadow double.

Next, the mother pulled out a flashlight and shined it at their feet. The girl watched curiously as her shadows soared high, then low, here, then there.

Finally, the mother took the girl out beneath the moonlight and just as the evening clouds filled the sky, the girl looked down and discovered she had no shadow at all.

'Do you know who you are now?' asked the mother.

'Of course!' said the girl. 'The one who never changes and is always here.'

. . . .

What never changes and is always here?

Afterall, it's been said, 'No person steps in the same river twice, for it's not the same river and they're not the same person.'

On one hand, this is true. A river is constantly changing. Each moment it's running by the shoreline, flowing with different water. We cannot stop it or hope to keep the same water here from one moment to the next.

And the 'us' that's stepping in the river is also changing. Our skin is change, our thoughts are change. Our height changes, our weight changes, our beliefs change, our roles and relationships change.

Yet, far beneath the surface, at the very heart of our being, there's a part of us that lives on—one that enters a stream at four and can return at forty.

This isn't groundbreaking. We each experientially *know* there is some part of us the hand of change has never reached. Whether we can speak to it or not, every person on the planet, consciously or unconsciously, senses that part of their 'I' remains just as youthful and unbroken at eighty as at eight.

What is this independent dimension?

What is this quality that is not bound by the movements of time or shaped by the conditions or circumstances of our lives?

BODY:
THE PHYSICAL YOU

Deep in the woods behind my high school there was an old, abandoned house. By the time my friends and I stumbled upon it, it was covered in mold and caved in on itself—but it used to be a host to some form of life. One could imagine it housing a family of two or five or however many for years. But it was clearly no longer in a condition for life. And each time we returned, we found it had collapsed more and more.

. . . .

Physical things change. In fact, we could just say 'things' change. A 'thing' is that which has a size or shape. It can be held, felt and perceived. And whether it slithers like a snake, leaps like a rabbit or is as cold and lifeless as a rock, the nature of it is change. A flower changes; an oak tree changes; a chair and a desk change and even the stars and planets cannot escape this. It doesn't matter whether a particular thing is oval or triangular, red or yellow or if it just got here or has been carrying on for some time—all things change.

A body is no different.

It's a seemingly solid shape. It stands six feet tall or five and three quarters and comes black or white or brown or yellow. And just as the old house behind my high school was bound to break down, the body is also. It has no timeless quality. If we are solely the shape of the body, we'll be living out the same wear and tear.

Of course, we may say, 'Yes, but without the body I wouldn't exist.'

On one level, this is certainly true. When the body goes, the mind goes. Our personality and all the worldly aspects of ourselves fall to the dirt—just like an old house. But the reason we value a house isn't for its walls and roof. The highest value for a house is found in the space between them. It's in the space where people eat and sleep and think and love. It's in the space where people take shelter and seek warmth and where life is happening. Imagine a house with no space and you imagine no house at all.

Within the walls of the body, there's a similar spaciousness. And it is the higher value. It's only that space that can house something timeless; that can house the 'us' not bound by change. And just as the walls and roof of a house fall down and its space goes free, we could imagine the space within the body doing the same. Perhaps it goes up or down or into some new form or state of formlessness. Who is to say?

We explore our inner space more in chapter three ('Coming Home through the Breath') and chapter four ('Coming Home through the Inner Body').

MIND:
THE PSYCHOLOGICAL YOU

The traffic on a highway is always changing. One moment, it's bustling with cars; the next, it's nearly empty. One moment, a Lamborghini and a Ferrari are racing by; another, a 2000 Honda hatchback and a garbage truck. If we had our way, perhaps we'd choose for there to be no traffic at all. Or perhaps we'd choose for the traffic to *only* be one particular car driving north at sixty five miles per hour. But traffic isn't a constant thing. Neither are our minds.

. . . .

One moment, your mind is full. It's rushing back and forth with all sorts of thoughts. It's honking so loud you can't even see straight. The next, it's nearly empty. It's not talking at all. One moment, it's thinking the most beautiful thought imaginable—time spent with loved ones or dreamscape vacation in the Alps. The next, it's weaving a Greek tragedy you can't seem to outrun.

We all know this is happening. We all know our thoughts are always changing. But few of us pull up a chair to see just how quickly it unfolds.

Imagine you are seeing a sunrise over the Atlantic—purple and pure. You're thinking about the sunrise, its reflection in the waters, its vibrance in the sky. At first, you're only thinking of what's here; the salty air; the easy breeze; the oranges and the purples and the pinks. But then what's here starts reminding you of something else. Some grander beach, of a girl or boy you kissed there. Then it reminds you of something you learned in grade school or of how cruel Christopher Columbus was or of something that isn't around or some happening that isn't now. The next thing you know, you're thinking about breakfast. Then dinner. Then breakfast for dinner and about how intolerable your life is and why things are never working out for you and how you're destined to die alone before coming full circle and thinking you really should make more time to enjoy beautiful sunrises like this one.

Most of us spend our lives in this state—living *as* the traffic. Hopping aboard one passing car after another—a Porsche, then a Yugo; a Lamborghini, then a dump truck. If we don't like our mental traffic, we can try changing our thoughts. We can read different books and trade out belief systems and try to *only* think about Lamborghini's and Ferraris. This can help smooth the flow of traffic. But the world is always throwing change at us. We're hot then we're cold, we're healthy then we're sick, we're up then we're down and everything in between. Naturally, all these changes show up in the mind. Naturally, the traffic changes also.

This is why there's a need for spirituality and meditation. Because only these dimensions can keep us from living like a passenger in our own minds. Only these can show us that passing cars, while glimmering and flashy, aren't 'us'—they're just an activity. They're birds fluttering through the inner sky. They aren't the sky. They aren't the subject, the noun; they're it's activity, it's verb. They aren't your *essence*; they're your karma, your process. When mind energy is in a rush hour of thought we miss this. We can't notice the gaps—the gaps in between cars and in between thinking. But just as the space of a house is more important than its walls, the gaps on a highway are more true than the traffic. It's the open lane, the empty space—the gap—*in which* the traffic appears. It's the gap that is the noun. Movements of mind are just fluttering verbs. We explore this more in depth in each of the following three chapters, most notably chapter five ('Coming Home through the Mind').

. . . .

You are not simply a storehouse of memories and food— and deep down, you know it.

'I am the shape of this body and I am the traffic of this mind.' Perhaps you can see how this isn't completely true, how it overlooks our essence for our shape and a noun for a verb.

Or perhaps you can at least imagine that there's a deeper reality, a deeper truth. We're often told about this truth. We're handed various ideas about ourselves, deeper ideas. But frequently, those ideas are simply that; ideas. And those who handed them to us are simply handing down what was handed to them. It isn't direct knowledge. It isn't a flower that grew in their garden—it came from someone else's.

So we may have ideas about some 'formless' essence—a soul, a spirit, energy or 'the Self'—but few of us are encouraged to seek the experience out for ourselves. So we believe or disbelieve various things and stake our claim in different traditions, but our experience of being *only* the shape of the body and the traffic of the mind continues. It's a persistent belief, a persistent experience.

And on one level, it's true. Just as leaves are prone to changing, but can still say, 'I am the tree', the body and the mind energy are also 'us'. They are 'you'. We might simply say that bodies are things we have; thoughts are things we do—but neither enters the river twice.

Who does?

AWARENESS:
THE SPIRITUAL YOU

For a second, press pause on religion. You can pick it back up soon. But whether you're religious or non-religious, for a moment, just set down your conclusions. See that prior to any belief system or interpretation, at the very heart of life, at the very beginning, life is spiritual. First and foremost, it is spiritual. It's not Jewish, not Buddhist, not Christian, not Hindu, not Muslim; spiritual. Spiritual in its essence, in its essential quality.

Look at a pine tree—stretching tall and high, swaying in the sunlight. It is pure life. When spring arrives, the pine will begin seeding. And though the seeds will be very small, very delicate, each seed will house the whole life energy of the pine. From there, a seed will fall to the earth and start growing into a seedling; then the seedling into an adolescent pine; then the adolescent pine into the towering tree. But across all its changing shapes and sizes, the life essence of the pine is unchanged. It is independent of shape, size and condition. It is dimensionless.

This is the nature of life. Just as you may have been born in a house in the country, moved into an apartment in the city and then settled into a home in the suburbs, the shapes which house life itself differ. For the pine, life moves from cone to seedling to sapling to tree. The houses change. One is the height of a mountain, the other can fit on your index finger. Both are *life*. The inner processes differ. At one stage, they're navigating the world for the house of the seed. At another, the house of a pine. Its *light of life*, its conscious essence, is unchanging. It is equally in the seed that fits on your index finger as the towering pine swaying in the moonlight—both house *I AM*.

. . . .

I AM is life. It's what's always here and now. And life is spiritual.

This isn't a statement of belief or religion. It's a certain quality of perception. Life is formless, thus, it assumes different shapes and looks out behind different faces. Life is timeless, thus, it lives in the first pine, the fiftieth and all the pines to come. Every spiritual teacher had this quality of perception. Every buddha or Jesus or Mohammad looked deeply and perceived this truth. The perception was the same. The routes they recommend we go vary. The routes are uniquely crafted by language, culture and the tuning of their hearts and minds. So the marketing and instruction manuals differ—they're for different audiences. But the starting point is *always* to become child-like, to renew our minds, to look again and see our original face. Because the initial perception and recognition is this—life is spiritual, life is timeless and at its heart, all life is one.

. . . .

You may say, 'Yes, but we're not just pine trees—we're people!'

True, a person is not a pine tree. A person is never housed in a pinecone, a seedling, a sapling and the rest. Instead, our essence dances from two cells to four cells to eight cells and on; from zygote, to embryo, to human being. From two cells we are now in the house of the body with the traffic of the mind. This traffic is simply the way the house relates to the world. Change the house and the relationship changes. A bird doesn't think like a fox, a fox doesn't think like a salmon and a boy doesn't think like a man. 'When I was a child I thought like a child. When I became an adult, I put the ways of childhood behind me.' But the true 'I'—that which 'lights' the body with life—is formless, timeless, spiritual. Again, not spiritual as in religious. Not spiritual as in the collective conditioning we hear attached to the word. Spiritual as in formless, timeless—and we each are that.

. . . .

When you hear claims that you're 'formless and timeless', it's easy to think, 'No, no, not me. I'm not that grand.' But most would say the sky is grand, the ocean is grand. This we can agree on.

But have you seen this? You step out into the evening and look up. The sky is vast and all-pervading—but easily it fits inside your mind. You fly over the ocean—great and blue—and look down. It's but a drop in your awareness. Both are so large. You can't hope to box them up. But effortlessly they rest in your mind.

There is a dimension in us that is grand, grander than skies and oceans. But we never touch it while living as the outer shell, while knowing only the changing elements of our lives—a body and a mind.

Being a body puts us in space and space creates distance. It separates a man from his wife, a brother from his sister, a person from their desires.

And being a mind puts you in time and living in time creates restlessness. It lures us out of the fulfilling waters of *being* and into a life of perpetual seeking, chasing and doing.

Living in a state of doing, the body gets gripped by compulsions and addictions. Living in an unending narrative *about* life, the mind spends its days trying to correct the past and improve the future.

To me, all immorality, bad habits and unwanted patterns of behavior arise from this. They arise from being lost amongst the outer shells of life and forgetting its essence. The result is greed, envy, lust, suffering and violence. In religious terms, we could say the result is 'Being separated from

God.' It's being cast into a world of separateness and change. One where life is suffering and death is inevitable.

Naturally, there is a longing to know the spiritual in the human family because deep within the recesses of our consciousness, there is a sense of the Eden that we've lost. There is a longing to 'return to God' and to a state of felt oneness and timelessness. To me, these are the qualities of a spiritual experience; oneness and timelessness—which is the experience of the formless essence of life itself.

. . . .

This is why Buddha's timeless call is 'remember'. Remember your being, your universalhood, your truth! Remember your essence, your nature, your Buddhahood!

Remember that you have made a home in different bodies—laid down in different cells and sinews, shapes and sizes—and wandered through different minds—watched different thought forms, preferences, memories, beliefs and ideas—you've remained. *I AM, consciousness, awareness* has remained. A spiritual life is keeping your finger on the pulse of this.

'YES, BUT...'

If the *'Spiritual You'* is there, why are we so unaware of it?

This is often the biggest obstacle to *truly* hearing this message. 'All of this sounds logical, desirable, but if it were real, surely I wouldn't have missed it.'

For most things, this is true. A wallet or a set of keys may go missing for an afternoon. But if it's *right there*, right in front of you, you're bound to stumble upon it sooner or later. Even without looking, it's bound to show up. But the *Spiritual You* isn't like wallets or car keys. The *Spiritual You* is a different kind of 'thing'. So even though it's obvious and apparent—even though it's always with us and always *is* us—it takes a different kind of looking. It takes a different kind of looking because it's sitting in the one place you can't see: you. So it's less like missing a wallet or car keys. It's more like a movie goer missing himself.

It's more like a movie goer who, in tirelessly watching the character in a movie searching for his wallet or car keys, forgets he's there. He gets so wrapped up in the movie that he forgets the place *from which* he's looking. And he starts feeling like quite a fantasy to himself. The idea of him as a movie watcher and not some character, some 'person' starts feeling very hippy, very 'woo woo'. Because he just can't seem to find himself. He's too close. He's too *It*.

So he ends up feeling like the two fish out at sea. The first turns to the second, 'Water sure is cold this morning.' And the second goes, 'What the hell is water?'

. . . .

We are most unaware of that which is closest to us. We often know more about the moon than we know ourselves. Afterall, we can watch it. It's over there. We know its shape, its color. How it's illuminating the night sky or hiding behind evening clouds. We know little about the one who watches. We know more about God than the one who watches. The human family has more knowledge about the one in whom they believe or disbelieve than the one doing the believing. I am not against seeking knowledge of other things—moons, clouds, atoms or God. All of these should be pursued and integrated. But a real scientist masters the microscope before lecturing on the slides; a real seeker knows themselves before seeking to know the nature of God or the world.

Of course, maybe we don't identify as a seeker. Or at least up until now we haven't. So maybe we don't give ourselves so much credit. The mind may say, 'It's possible for me to have missed this, but not my brother, not my father—not my family and my community and the human family at large. So surely if this were true, *someone* would be broadcasting it.'

Certainly. And it is being broadcasted. It's being broadcasted by people and it's being broadcasted by the world, by *life*. But each radio has its own responsibility also. It must meet the broadcast half-way. It must tune in. And the collective mind hasn't tuned in. They aren't tuning into the station of *Self*-knowing or unity consciousness. To this point in history, the collective mind is tuned into the other stations. Stations of individualism and entertainment; industry and economics; science and matter. So we keep picking up the same world and recycling the same perspectives. This isn't because the higher station, the higher reality doesn't exist or isn't being shared. It's because it's fallen outside of the collective awareness. The world is filled with things outside of our awareness.

. . . .

Butterflies fluttering through a garden see a different world than you see. Their world is all ultraviolet, all purples and oranges and pinks. But as far as detail goes, they're impaired flyers. They're nearly blind. They cannot see the nuances of the flower petal or the different shades of green in the magnolia leaf. Their vision is grander, more colorful, but more broad strokes. It's less realism, more impressionism. You try to tell a butterfly there's more to their reality, that there are more details and more distinctions than purples and pinks and the rest, they won't believe you—because for them it isn't true. It doesn't matter which butterfly you approach. They are all the same. One butterfly's mind is a reflection of all the millions of butterfly minds. They all filter the world through the same field of awareness, the same eyes and the same mind, just multiplied. So what one misses, they all miss.

It's the same with the human family. We have distinct bodies and minds, but share a field of awareness. It's amazingly detailed. It's hyper-realism compared to the butterfly's, filled with all sorts of dazzling shades and nuances. And because of all the endless details, a sort of collective story about them arises. Because no single mind can be an expert on all of it. There's too much. There's too many separate things for one lifetime. So I take your word about what's over that ridge and you take my word about who's in the valley. We'll both take Frank's word about the bad mushrooms and we're still not sure about what Carl called those chickens but we'll pass it down to the kids anyway. And their kids. And their kids.

Quickly, there starts to arise a collective conditioning, a collective story. Which is an agreed upon map of reality. Our field of awareness gets layered with language and education and various belief systems and ideologies to affirm the map, all of which shape the world we see.

And there's the rub. A butterfly's blindness is his eyes and a human being's blindness is his conditioning. Because most of us don't see the world—we see our thought-world, our conditioning. We see our internal map. Our map about what's right and what's wrong and who's in charge.

We've made room for all of these things. But the collective internal map has yet to make space for the one who watches, for the higher reality. So it appears missing. Telling most of us otherwise is just like telling a butterfly there's more to reality, to existence. It seems like there's only two things she can do with that: believe or disbelieve. Take it on faith one way or the other.

So if you're reading all this about the *Spiritual You* and it agrees with your internal map, you agree with it. And if not, then not. But there's a key distinction—the butterfly's body and mind cannot perceive the missing reality. Though the details are plainly there, it is an impossibility. They don't have the proper instruments.

A human being's body and mind are different. It is the perfect instrument—it is made in 'God's image'. It *can* know itself. It can touch the missing reality.

So for someone *really* interested in what's true, there's no taking it on faith. There's no believing or disbelieving. At first, these can be useful. Anyone who follows Jesus or Buddha or any spiritual figure is asked to believe. Belief is what draws you to the foot of the master. It's what gets your heart running and your feet following. So belief is useful. It's a good launch site. But it's no destination. In spirituality, there's only one destination: come and experience, come and *know*.

UNBOXING THE SPIRITUAL YOU

Mentally 'getting this' can be a first step. But it doesn't really get us any closer to *experiencing* ourselves *as it*. It doesn't make the house and the traffic any less convincing or the spiritual 'I' anymore tangible. And in many ways, it shouldn't. Spirituality is non-tangible. It's like the sky or the air; space or 'gaps'. None of these are actual 'things'. Which is to say, the sky isn't an object. Space isn't an object. The sky isn't a rock and space isn't a sweet potato. They aren't so easily held by the mind. Without the label 'sky' or 'space', we'd hardly be aware that either exist, much less be able to talk about them.

So it helps us approach something by labeling it—even if the sky, space or spirituality isn't *exactly* a 'thing' at all.

What names have been used for the Spiritual You?

In western faiths, we often hear it simply called 'spirit'. It's the 'God breathed' essence. 'God took the dirt (body), breathed in life (spirit) and created a living being (soul).' Some may call the Spiritual You the 'soul' as well, though soul often implies a sense of individuality—as in, there's your soul, your mother's soul, your father's soul and on. Spirit doesn't discriminate—there's just *spirit*. So spirit is closer to the spiritual self. But certainly both point us towards the deeper dimension. So if the word 'soul' resonates, feel free to use it.

In eastern faiths, we often hear it called Atman or simply the 'Self'. It's a different label but the same essence as spirit.

Still, others call it *Tao, Buddha nature or Christ within*. If all of these carry too much baggage, we can also say it is simply *consciousness, source, being, awareness* or *I AM*. All of this vocabulary is pointing to the formless life energy—not to the shape of the body or the traffic of the mind, but to the *light of life* which enters the stream at four and returns at forty,.

Awareness, Self, presence, source, the deeper 'I', being, consciousness, I AM, light of life—these names are used throughout this book. But again, don't overvalue the vocabulary. Overvaluing vocabulary is the surest way to miss the experience.

. . . .

Once, a father told his daughter of a lovely bird—a blue and yellow finch that sang a beautiful song. The daughter loved her father's tale of the bird. She could hardly sleep that night, thinking about it. The next day, the daughter gets out of bed and continues her thinking, brushing her teeth, putting on her clothes, eating her breakfast, thinking about the bird, imagining its colors, its song. The bus for school arrives and she goes out the front door, still thinking about the bird. And in her thinking about it, she misses the very bird sitting on the rooftop, just overhead. She misses it because it doesn't align with her conditioning. It's out of alignment with her internal map. So it's a little less blue than her ideas about it, it's a little more yellow than her beliefs about it. And the talking in her head over both keep her from hearing its song.

A name is a signpost. It points in the direction of something. But keep looking at the sign and we miss why it's there.

Awareness, presence, the deeper 'I', source, being, I AM, light of life, Self; what we're doing with these labels is bringing more awareness to the nameless essence of life. We're drawing attention away from our sense of self based on the outer shells. Based on our body, roles, relationships and worldly achievements and towards the formless life energy; away from an 'I' that is shaped by beliefs and thoughts and feelings and into the field of aware presence.

THE RETURN TO SPIRIT: A HAPPY UNRAVELING

So how can we know the *light of life?* How can we sink beneath the changing leaves of body and mind and return to the root of our *being?*

Just as a rubber band ball is too tightly wound for us to know what lies at its center, so we are wound so tight that we don't know what lies at our own. The field of body and mind appears like a giant, tangled web.

Perhaps this web feels like a binding, inescapable knot. One that closes off our whole being. And no matter how we hack away at it or twist and turn we can't seem to wrangle free. Or perhaps it's more subtle. It's more like a dripping faucet, more happening in the background. But whether it's a dull whisper or a smothering constraint, it's rather persistent. Outside of life's brief intermissions, the intermissions of sex and laughter, entertainment and substances, we go on carrying this tension around.

This is the reality most of us live in—tension isn't something we have; tension is our sense of self.

And even meditative minds say, 'I've looked for something else, but it doesn't exist. My 'space' and 'gaps' aren't big enough, aren't wide enough. And even in them, I still feel this tension.'

How to see beyond it?

. . . .

Once, a Sufi master was asked how to find the *Self*, how to find peace. He said, 'One should start by taking a nap.'

Deep sleep is a dissolving of the mind into its source. Which is to say, the collapse of mental traffic, conscious, subconscious and unconscious; the traffic of today, yesterday and the traffic that came pre-wired, pre-installed.

Self-realization is the art of being dissolved with the lights on.

So being aware of deep sleep is a great aid. It's a mirror for our deepest *Self,* for pure *awareness.* Particularly if we can't find any gaps or any space in waking life. Because each time we fall deeply asleep, we come *home.* And what is there but peace? Beneath all the bands of resistance; peace, a peace that surpasses understanding.

It doesn't matter if we have a saintly mind or a sinful mind, a loving mind or a hateful mind. When deep sleep comes, it comes for all. In deep sleep, there is no bad man and there is no good man, no believing man and no disbelieving man, no Jesus and no Judas. There is only the aliveness of *being* or awareness. The *I AM* free of the thinker an world.

This *I AM* is not just the quality shared between the boy and man who enter the stream in different seasons. This quality disrobes itself nightly, independent of when and where.

In days of ecstasy and youth, when we fall into deep sleep, it reveals itself. We touch the space of pure timelessness, formlessness and peace. This is *I Am.* In seasons of inescapable trauma and loss—ones where each hour seems to drag on for months—the same space is unveiled.

. . . .

The mind may think we are *least* ourselves in deep sleep— that we're the least 'us' when the mind is off.

Yet, what is deep sleep other than you going to the ground floor of yourself? And what is the ground floor of yourself but that upon which all of you is built?

So it's not that in deep sleep you are not 'yourself'. In deep sleep you are not slipping out of 'you'; you are falling into *you* without the distractions. You are being the blank screen without any movie playing. Without any changing story about a character or a drama or a world.

'Spiritual awakening' is this screen 'waking up' to itself. Waking up with the projector running, with the lights on and the movie there. Which is waking up to the primary reality, the timeless, shared reality of our deepest *being*. It's this reality that all religious teachers refer to when they say, 'I'—because it's simply the truth of 'I', whether we know it or not.

This all sounds non-rational to the thinking mind. It sounds like fantasy. All the while, anyone who has gone deeply enough inward has already discovered this.

. . . .

As far as this book goes, the discovery can happen two ways. The first is through patience and ease.

Imagine you are overlooking a choppy lake—tossing and muddy. If you want to know its depths, you cannot force it.

You cannot grab a paddle or a buoy and flatten the water down. This simply creates less clarity, more waves. To see the depths, you must remain patient and peaceful. The same applies to seeing your own.

If we ease the breath (Chapter 3), relax the body (Chapter 4) or soften the mind (Chapter 5), more and more clarity arises. If we remain conscious in this process, we can glimpse the deeper waters. This glimpsing is gradual. Through a devotion to ease, slowly who we are becomes more and more obvious. This is one method. It's more common, more earthy. It's more for sensory types.

But there is a second way to glimpse the bottom: you throw off your constraints, abandon the world and take a dive. You release the body and mind energies entirely and dive inward. And if we dive inward and start looking closely enough at the breath, going deeply enough into the body or genuinely investigating the nature of the mind, the same depths are revealed. This path is more intuitive. It's less a gradual unfolding, more an unmasking. We see that the choppy waves and muddy surface are extensions of us. They speak to the possibilities and potentials of the deep, but they're less true to our enduring nature.

The two paths work together. It's easier to get to the bottom when the surface is calm. And it's easier to understand the surface when the bottom is revealed. The following chapters join hands so that both might be made clear and accessible.

DIRECTLY HOME

3 COMING HOME THROUGH THE BREATH

Once, Mrs. White's sixth grade class was given a new bicycle. It was a perfect machine, state-of-the-art. But before the opening bell, a group of ninth graders decided they'd break it in. They saw the note, 'For Mrs. White's sixth grade class' and hopped on anyway. Instantly, the seat bowed. They raced through the courtyard, popping wheelies. A peddle cracked. They sped through the parking lot, zipped through three lanes of traffic and crashed straight into the back of Mrs. White's school bus. The sixth graders piled out of the bus, 'Hey, what happened to our bicycle?'

'That bicycle's old news…' said the ninth graders, marching back to school. 'But we hear Mrs. Kelly's seventh grader's got a brand new six-speed!'

. . . .

Breath is like a worn-out bicycle—it's old news. In meditative circles, there's no topic more overplayed. It's that one song on the radio you can't seem to get away from. The first time it came on, it was okay. But our ears can only hear something so many times before our hearts stop listening. And when they do, the song can still be thought about, it can be appreciated mentally, but it can no longer be *felt* or experienced. Much like a magic trick we've seen one too many times, the mind thinks, 'Oh, I know this thing. I've ridden this bike. Next!'

If your mind is doing this with the topic 'breath', I'd invite you to drop a few conclusions. Drop as many as feels reasonable and begin feeling into the words with your heart.

Don't worry over how you could maintain an awareness of the breath or your failures in the past to do so or your smaller and larger doubts. All of these are the limitations of the mind. Drop them and start feeling for what breath is right now because with a little awareness, it is so multifunctional. With a little awareness and a little willingness, you will find it is filled with so much potential.

Physically, breath is a great conductor of energy. It can reroute the whole energy of the body. It can open up new pathways for vitality and awareness to start flowing. And flow is the end of tension. When breath energy is truly flowing, physical tensions start dropping. Simply through a change in breathing, you can start feeling your frequency shift. Which is to say you can feel your body becoming lighter, more open and expansive. You can start feeling a lifting quality instead of a downward pull. This is simply the physical potential.

Psychologically, breath starts emptying the mind. Because as a body becomes lighter, thoughts become lighter. If you are willing to drop your physical tensions, you can start dropping your mental tensions. And wherever you are in the world, you will find less of it in you.

And as these two potentials are happening—the lifting of the body and mind—you can touch the spiritual potential, the deeper potential. Because breath energy is less material, less physical than nearly every other object of awareness. It is less material than our thoughts of cars and women or work and relationships or becoming or achieving something. It is even less material than our thoughts about God. Because most of our thoughts about God are so weighed down with descriptions. Descriptions always lead us back into the world because descriptions are for worldly things, not so much for the Infinite. They are more for rocks, trees and tabletops. They are less for the boundless, the unfathomable, the unending. Naturally, the more describable we feel something is, the less spiritual potential it has, because descriptions don't open the mind—they don't unify or expand the mind—they take up space in the mind.

So for many, the breath is the most spiritual gateway available. Breath cannot *truly* be described. It cannot take up space—it creates spaciousness.

Naturally, breath becomes a cliché because it is so versatile and available. No matter who we are, what we believe or where we come from, it's there. It's always on and always going.

For those with the courage to endure the initial discomfort that comes from removing the mind from the world, breath is always a friend. It is the most accessible way to create a physical and psychological healing and to discover spiritual awareness. No belief is necessary, only exploration.

CHECKING THE TIRES

How are you feeling right now? Begin breathing and see. If you're feeling nasty or angry or depressed, where is your breath?

Start becoming more and more aware of it. When we add a drop of awareness to the breath, we see it is often in line with our state. They go together.

If our state is closed off, our breath has become closed off. If we are feeling out of rhythm, our breath has lost its rhythm. And the further out of rhythm our breathing falls, the more out of rhythm we fall with the world. Our hearts start growing harder, less yielding. Our minds start growing defensive and withdrawn.

Sometimes, our state drags the breath down and other times our breath does the pulling. But one never moves without the other. As we start becoming aware, we can see it happening the other way, too. If in this moment we sweeten—we feel peaceful and content—how is our breathing? It's also in line with our state. Our breathing is relaxed, pure and open. If it isn't, the sweetness won't last for long.

This is only a short exploration, but it reveals a powerful connection. It shows how our breath energy and our life energy are joined. It shows how any moment we begin addressing our breath, we begin addressing our quality of life. This is why in Sanskrit breath and life share one name: 'prana'. They are inescapably linked.

So yes, breath might be old news. It might be an old bicycle we've tired of riding. The thinking mind says, 'Don't go back there, what we need is something else!' But unlike Mrs. White's bicycle, if the way we're breathing is damaged, turning to something else won't help. Breathing needs to be repaired—it needs to flow naturally—otherwise who would enjoy the ride? It will be too uncomfortable.

. . . .

The more unnatural anything becomes, the more discomfort is there. To me, unnaturalness and discomfort are synonyms. Only when we're living against what's natural does discomfort come knocking. And it comes knocking for our benefit.

We have no problem believing this when it applies to the body. When the stove is burning and our hand grazes the pan, we're quick to recoil. Because the relief is immediate, our response is immediate.

Emotional and mental discomfort arise for a similar purpose. They are there to nurture us and bring us back to a place suitable for life. The relief is just a little more delayed, but the discomfort is still life saying the same thing; 'You've gone astray!'. It is happiness saying, 'I'm not that way, you're getting colder.'

The next step is simple. If you're riding along and suddenly your bike starts rattling, you don't keep pedaling like things are normal. Nor do you head straight to the bike shop. You pause and check if the tires are flat.

Many of the discomforts we face are similar; it's our response that's different. To me, we're too quick to call our discomfort our reality and too inclined to run to the liquor store, the dispensary and the pharmacist.

But flat tires and human beings aren't so different. Often, they're in need of the same two things.

AWARENESS AND SPACE

Once, a man was walking through a forest. Simply walking, enjoying the day. Suddenly, out of nowhere, he was struck by a sharp object—an arrow hit him in the back. Immense pain entered his awareness. He started running and as he was running, he began thinking of the pain, the discomfort. Naturally, the pain turned to misery. He got home and the misery expanded. His mind wanted to know who, how, what and why. It couldn't let go of the questions. This is how a wave of pain turns into a storm of suffering. Suffering is the second arrow. And the second cuts deeper than the first. After all, the pain is just a sensation. Even though the arrow pierces the skin, it is still just surface level. But suffering reaches the heart. It bleeds out of the mind and swallows you.

This story is from the Buddha. It's a reminder that we can't always avoid the first arrow. We can be whatever person and live whatever type of life we want; pain still finds us. But pain is no great problem. The greatest victories of life are won through pain. The sweetest rewards are measured by the pains endured to achieve them. And life itself is born out of pain. Children are won through the pain of childbirth. Pain is how new generations announce their arrival. Knowing this, one can at least make room for the first arrows. But when we hear them cutting through the wind and close our eyes, we miss a great opportunity. It's the opportunity to glimpse who is holding the second bow. At no other time is the perpetrator available. And when we create a little space, we can see him. We can observe pain entering the body through one door and hear the mind drawing back its bow at the other.

It is meeting pain with violence that creates misery. And as we start fighting and resisting pain, the mind turns to the breath and calls for reinforcements. If our awareness is lacking, our inhale and exhale start falling to the minimum. They amplify the problem. If that which is giving us life is at the minimum, naturally we start feeling reduced. More arrows

And is it any wonder why? The more limited our breathing, the more we take on the qualities of misery. Depression is a constricting of the throat, the chest and the mind. If we are depressed, we feel ourselves as weighty, contracted and withdrawn. Anger is a clinching of the shoulders, the hands, the lungs. If we give rise to anger, we tense up.

Peace is the opposite; a total relaxation and release. Joy is even further; spaciousness, openness, expansion.

The opportunity to be relaxed and spacious is always in front of us. With a little awareness, it can begin with the next inhale. The more natural and expansive the inhale, the more we invite our body, mind and heart to open, to flower. And with the same awareness, the invitation will grow through the release. The more completely and effortlessly we release breath energy, the more completely and effortlessly we release our tensions. Slowly, the mind finds its equilibrium.

It may take practice for us to find our equilibrium. The desire for peace must grow larger than our desire for justice. And you might be surprised to find this desire for peace requires muscle memory. It requires choosing peace over preferences and ease over victimhood. But learning the art of peace is the same as mastering the piano or swinging golf clubs—through practice, muscle memory is born. It isn't always fun, but it arrives. And with the muscle memory of choosing ease over tension, peace becomes a state of effortless embodiment. It arrives more and more and the second arrows, less and less.

. . . .

You may be thinking, 'Perhaps this is true, but this doesn't have much to do with a 'Spiritual You'—with awareness or 'timelessness and oneness'.

No, not on the surface. But the more closed a door is the less you can see what's on the other side. Naturally, if what's giving you life is a little closed off, it will be difficult to glimpse the greater life within you. This is to say, the more tense and unnatural our breathing, the more likely we are to *only* have eyes for the outer shells—our body, mind and the world. We are likely to only have eyes for the outer shells because they will constantly be asking for our attention.

The body and mind will constantly be reminding us that something is off. Feeling limited is something being off. Feeling reduced and tense and withdrawn is something being off. And as long as something is off, it will feel like something needs doing. It will feel like something needs fixing and repairing. Something needs to be acquired and some higher state of comfort and accomplishment must be worked out before peace is possible.

With awareness, we begin seeing this more and more clearly. We begin understanding how the way we inhabit the body, mind and breath keeps us identified with the outer shell. And with space, we start creating more and more room to see what's beyond it. The greater the awareness and the greater the space, the wider the door can swing open.

FULL BODY BREATHING

True spaciousness is not just an opening of the lungs and an emptying of the mind. It is a more total happening—it includes our whole being.

Imagine you are looking at a tree—a great water oak on a street corner. You look to its green leaves, its flowing branches. You feel its great trunk and marvel over its roots. You think, 'There are the leaves, there are the branches and there the trunk and roots.' But this is the mind's reality. In ultimate reality, there are no separate parts, only the one tree. The separate parts are an idea in the mind. Dividing up is the mind's business.

The truth is that the tree is simply one happening. It does not think of itself as root, trunk, leaf, branch. It did not think, 'Okay, today I am a root, tomorrow I will grow a trunk, then at some point in the distant future, I hope to grow a branch.' The tree is a seamless flowing of energy. It is one consciousness.

All beings are one flowing consciousness. When we divide ourselves into body, mind and spirit, this is simply to gain an initial understanding. If all we know of the oak tree is its leaves, it's helpful to make a distinction between leaves and roots. Without the initial distinction, we will never touch the deeper truth. We will fear for the fragility and the nakedness of the leaves and think the whole oak is in danger of toppling over at any moment. It's only through knowing the roots that we can arrive at peace. But once there is an awareness of the roots, then full integration must happen.

When breath energy flows in a circular motion through the body, we start becoming like the water oak; integrated and whole. This is what is meant by yoga.

Yoga is not posture and motion. Yoga means union. Yoga means all your energies are flowing as one. We explore this more in the next chapter ('Coming Home through the Inner Body'), but this flowing cannot happen when breath is shallow, when it reaches only the upper half and is cut off from the lower.

This cutting off from the lower reflects the movement of the human family, from being fully embodied to being mind-run. Imagine, what would happen if the water oak cut itself off from its roots. Quickly, it would start dying. This is what happens to all life when it begins living partially.

Humankind is largely defined by this partiality. Thus, yoga comes about. We have gone from being one seamless flowing, like the water oak, to being a crowd. Our minds are against our hearts. Our hearts are against our bodies. Our logic against our passions and our intellect against our love. Yoga breaks the dam. It places the mind, the heart and the body together and starts returning us to the proper flow. This is simply a return to the original oneness of Self.

This happens on three levels: spacious breathing; witnessing; resting in the gap.

. . . .

The First; breathe spaciously.

As you breathe, feel the incoming breath softening the body, opening the body. And as the body opens, feel your awareness opening also as if being drawn into the room. If you like, you can ease the inhale down the spine. And at it's peak, gently release it the way it came.

Don't get stuck on the nuts and bolts—where to place the mind and how to guide the breath. These are just suggestions. Simply make gentle, spacious breathing the aim. Breathing that flows beyond the body and fills the spaces around you.

At first, we make this conscious, which is to say that at first, we are making breath happen. When it finds its rhythm, we make it unconscious; we allow breathing to happen to us. We allow the body to breathe on its own—gently and spaciously in us and through us. This alone creates a great trance.

And the second; be a witness.

As breath finds its rhythm, just watch. Become a witness, just allowing a drop of awareness to rest on the breath. This witnessing will begin creating a deeper harmony. Just as a driver looking at a passing building will find himself drifting in its direction, whatever we observe, we move towards. If we watch something in harmony, we take on its qualities. We sit with a child, we become child-like. We spend time barefooted in the garden, we start flowering. And even more so when what we observe is dancing within us. The qualities happen more totally. The harmony is louder. As we watch breath energy falling in tune, we fall in tune, just by witnessing it.

But perhaps at first, witnessing seems to take a great effort. We feel like we're trying to force the highway of the mind to slow down, but cars keep whizzing by—cars of yesterday and tomorrow and cars of responsibilities and lunch and all sorts of things. This is natural. Thoughts are going to come and thoughts are going to go and it's fine. It's not our choice. Our choice is simply to be allowing, to relax.

So when the mind hops in a passing car and you become aware, don't slam on the breaks. This resistance simply creates more traffic, less space. Simply relax. Whether you've been in the car for two seconds, ten seconds or five minutes—smile. Breathe into the space of the room and return to being a loving witness.

In time, if we keep a strong intention, a strong 'why', a background of awareness will start resting upon the breath naturally.

So first, begin breathing spaciously, beyond the body. Then allow it to happen and be a witness.

And the third level; rest in the gap.

You stay with the breath, witnessing. Perhaps you do so throughout the day or just in the morning or evening as you're lying in bed. You tune out the radio of thought and simply arrange your antenna to only pick up the breath.

While doing this, as the inhale reaches its peak, pause. Be still. Become more alert and watchful. When you know what happens at the turn of each breath the silence of life becomes available. Because when the breath reaches its peak, just there at the turn—after the inhale and before the exhale—there is a gap. When you become conscious in this gap, the door cracks open and you can glimpse the other side.

Notice how when you pause within the gap, the mind stops more totally. Thought forms disappear. The movement of the mind is connected to the movement of the breath.

When there is a moment of no breath energy, if you have a clean consciousness—just there in the gap—you experience a death. Not you as a body or a presence, but you as an ego, you as a smaller self. Your story dies, your drama dies, your self-possession dies. You touch something changeless, something *now*.

RENOUNCING BACK TO ABUNDANCE

At first, coming home through the breath might not offer any great reward. In fact, it may feels utterly mundane, utterly dismissible—just like pausing in the gap. So surely we're missing something. Surely we need to keep asking around because gaps and *now* don't always look like freedom or oneness and timelessness. They don't always seem to live up to the marketing.

Once, a great treasure was rumored to be in the attic of a monastery. The Father said that the first monk to retrieve it would be blessed for decades to come. Each night, a monk would tip toe out of bed and climb up the rickety ladder to the attic, hoping for a blessing. And each night, he would fall back down, shrieking in terror. On a certain night, Friar Lawrence came to the Father. 'Father, each night for ten years a new monk has climbed into the attic. And each night, I wake to hear his shrieking. Is this the devil's work?' The Father didn't say a word. He took Friar Lawrence by the hand, led him across the monastery and to the foot of the rickety ladder. There, he stopped a few paces short, opened the nearby fuse box and pointed to a switch labeled 'attic.' The Father flipped the switch. Instantly, a scream of terror filled the air and a monk, covered head to toe in cobwebs, fell from the ceiling. 'Monks are happy to chase a blessing,' said the Father, drawing another number on the wall. 'But I've yet to find one that'll clean that attic.'

Looking in the gap is just like flicking on the lights—it shows us what's there, but it doesn't always clean the attic. It doesn't clear the cobwebs. Deep in the unconscious, the cobwebs of attachment, loss and lack can carry right along. Cleaning them takes a deeper devotion. Because if we've been living unconsciously, unaware, turning the lights on can reveal many horrors. It can reveal all the reasons we turned the lights out in the first place. It can show us all the things we've been avoiding, all the traumatic stories of unworthiness and loss we've been hoping to forget.

So if we're just starting out, finding peace in the inner room can often feel quite impossible. Perhaps it happens once or twice. Perhaps there's an initial 'Ah ha'. Still, it doesn't live up to the marketing.

This happens when our minds have gotten filled up with the world. When we're used to carrying strong worldly attachments and worldly needs.

This is why Christ says, 'It's easier for a camel to go through the eye of a needle than it is for a rich man to enter the Kingdom of God.' You can't enter the Kingdom of God when you have your own kingdom living behind your eyes. And a rich man is too busy chasing his own kingdom. He can't enter the spiritual. He possesses more than what is needed and in his possessiveness, he can't find his Self. He can't find the child in him that's content with little. He can't find the richness of openness, spaciousness and awareness.

So the rich man is really hiding a great secret. A secret from himself and from the world. The secret that he is really just a poor man pretending to be a rich man. Inwardly, he is really more a beggar. After all, only a beggar needs money. It's not a lack of money, but the presence of need that makes one poor.

. . . .

All of us have our poverties, things we've begun carrying a sense of lack over. It's not a lack we entered the world with, but a lack we acquired along the way. This is why the first call of religion is to take a step back and become child-like. Because all the riches in the world can't afford the magic of a beginner's mind—which is a mind that can see 'the Kingdom', which can see ultimate reality.

So the call isn't for religiousness or knowledge. The call is to become spacious, to become renewed. The call is to renounce back to abundance. That's what true breath awareness is—a renouncing. Not a renouncing of anything *in* the world—our paycheck, our family or our lifestyle. It's a renouncing of being *of* the world. It's a renouncing of all the bricks that shape our mental walls, which are walls that lock us out from presence, existence and God.

Each method in this book is aimed at this, aimed at renouncing back to abundance. They can be taken as far as we want.

We can renounce a few thoughts and turn our mind to the breath. We can see the state change that's possible. And this can bring renewed agency and ease. If this is all we want, we should be honest with ourselves. We should accept where we are on the journey and the desire on our hearts. But know that this isn't spirituality or Self-realization. It can start the momentum. It can create changes. I celebrate those changes and the devotion to them. But they aren't realization.

For the realization there will have to grow a deeper ease, a deeper clarity. To begin growing this clarity through breath, there are three steps: One, breathe intimately, spaciously. Make it conscious and then allow it to flow naturally. Two, be the witness, observe. Three, be alert in the gap—rest in the gap.

The more we give ourselves to any of the three, even any of the three in isolation, the more we're renouncing. The more space enters our lives. Pain still happens. It will rob the body of its beauty and youth. But we will be more and more free from a story about it. Gradually, our minds will become cleaner and cleaner and our depths more and more crystallized. The *light of life* will be more and more obvious.

From there, we can begin building the reality of our choice. That's the gift of returning to spaciousness, to an empty room—we can arrange it however it suits us. We can express it however we choose. Naturally, the more clearly we see the part of us that is unconditioned, the more say we have in our conditioning.

BREATH PRACTICE

Erin could feel her husband pacing in the backyard, but couldn't bring herself to put the car in park. Every night for three months she'd been coming home to an argument.

'Why is he so difficult?' She wondered, rolling the faded wedding band around her finger. Exhausted, she slunk into the driver's seat and took a deep breath. 'How long are we gonna do this?'

She dropped the steering wheel from her hands and let the air spill out of her lungs. For the briefest moment, she paused. The questions faded. In their place, a faint stillness appeared. Quickly, her mind began stirring and she turned back to the problem; 'Why is he *so difficult?*'

Replays of long fights and late nights surfaced. He could never seem to accept her family or her background and she could never seem to accept his judgment. She'd begun to feel that no amount of therapy could fix it. But instead of giving her attention to the replays and the headaches, she let go further, reclining into the driver's seat and taking a deeper, calmer breath. Once again, the question faded.

A light hush fell over her. It started slowly, subtly trickling down her neck and washing across her shoulders. Her arms relaxed, her jaw unhinged and her eyes softened. Erin didn't resist the experience—she was tired of resisting. She didn't jump to intellectualize what was happening or rush to justify her problems. Instead, she gave herself to the moment. And as her breathing steadied, her whole body seemed to open. All the tension she'd been carrying for months began softening, spilling out from her chest, over her waist and down into the driver's seat.

She sat there, quietly observing her breath. For a third time, her mind stirred; 'Why is he *always so difficult?*'

Again, she turned her attention inward, through the thought, breathing in more purely, more totally. Suddenly, a hush fell over the car. It was easy, inviting. She began noticing all the sounds around her. A laughing child in a neighbor's lawn, a fluttering bird swooping over a nearby pine and a summer breeze blowing through its branches. With her attention turned away from thought, she could hear it all. And the purer she breathed and listened, the more her mind settled. A choiceless peace arose. She turned to meet it.

Taking a deep, easeful breath—through her chest, into her legs and spreading it down and out into the car—she paused at the bottom; alert and present. For the first time in her life, she felt a spaciousness, an openness in her body and mind. This openness was not limited or touched by thoughts of the past or future. This openness felt deeper than thought, deeper than the 'her' her coworkers knew, her husband knew—deeper even than she knew.

Slowly, she released the air before gently inviting it back and pausing at the turn. The spaciousness grew clearer, cleaner. And with this new clarity, she felt an effortless gratitude, a sense of pure life and pure presence that she had long forgotten.

'How have I missed this?' The thought arose.

She briefly considered it before inhaling and watching it pass. Once again, she became aware of the inner spaciousness, the gentle, nurturing source of her life. Some moments passed before a thoughtless realization stirred.

'This is *me,*' Erin felt.

Settling into her Self, she let the realization in deeper. After a few moments, the familiar sound of her husband's boots on evening pavement met the air. She savored one last easeful breath, centering herself in the thoughtless peace of her life, this moment and the space they both call home.

For the first time in weeks, a light smile lifted her lips. She opened her eyes and they found her husband's.

Turning off the car, she stepped out to greet him.

4 COMING HOME THROUGH THE INNER BODY

Once, there was a village lost in a thick fog. The fog was so dense the sun couldn't break through and stood so long that generations came and went never seeing its light.

On a certain day, a traveler stumbled in. He felt great compassion for the villagers—they were living in such darkness. He went to the chief and told him of a nearby river over which the sun was always shining. The chief thought surely they must see for themselves.

They set out for the river's edge and after a short hike, heard the rushing waters. With no one who could swim, the chief decided he would dig his way across.

'Quick! Get me my shovel and then we will see!' Demanded the chief, fearlessly.

'Then we will see! Then we will see!' chanted the villagers, handing over the shovel. The chief dug into the earth deeper and deeper until the spade hit metal. He turned to the villagers.

'Quick! Get me my pickaxe and then we will see!'

'Then we will see! Then we will see!' chanted the villagers, lowering the pickaxe. The chief hacked and hacked until the metal cracked clean open. The smell of rotten eggs met the air. Undeterred, he climbed inside and found a tunnel filled with a foul sludge.

'Quick! Get me the matches and then we will see!'

'Then we will see! Then we will see!' roared the villagers, lowering down the matches.

With great intensity, the chief reared back and struck the match. Instantly, a loud explosion filled the air, followed by the chief, soaring over the river in a ball of flames.

The villagers were stunned; 'What had become of the chief?' They fell into a deep hush. Just then, a voice stirred from the other side.

'I've seen the light!' Shouted the chief, hobbling down the shoreline and back across a bridge. 'Now we will see!'

'Now we will see! Now we will see!' The entire village chanted, before the chief settled them down.

'What to do now?' asked a villager. The chief leaned against the bridge, deep in thought.

'Follow me!' He shouted, limping off the bridge and marching back to the village. 'We need more matches!'

. . . .

The further away something seems, the more we feel a great effort is needed to get there. So naturally when it comes to things like peace and touching a sense of 'home' we have a hard time believing they can be so *here*.

Afterall, they seem very far from the normal human experience. They seem like a distant star on the horizon— faint and subtle. Surely, many miles separate us from its warmth and glow. Surely, first we need to strategize and plan or acquire some other tool or knowledge before we can get there. It can't be realized and experienced simply by going more into what's right here.

But when we use words like 'realized' and 'experience' what are we referring to?

We're not referring to reading some words or having some new thoughts to think about or gathering up something that's somewhere else. We're referring to realizing and experiencing something that is happening *right here;* experiencing the mountain ridge as brand new, feeling into the morning breeze, directly, clearly, as if for the first time. We're referring to having a new discovery about here, about *life*.

We can't discover the deeper reality of here while turning elsewhere. The more we turn elsewhere, the more we risk being like the chief. We have the right intention. We're longing to get to the light. We're longing for happiness. It's a good longing. The longing is right. But we're so wrapped up in our own thinking and strategizing about how to get there that our eyes grow blind to what's here.

This is why in Zen they have a saying; 'If you can't find the truth here, where else do you expect to find it?' Religiously, we could reinterpret, 'If you can't find God here, where else could He be?'

Both of these sayings are invitations to steer the mind back *home*. Which is the aim of spiritual life. This is why breath is a powerful medium. It's life, it's always here and it's always without form, always 'spiritual'. But it's not the only way. By crossing the bridge from body to *beingness*, we can glimpse the light as well.

TOUCHING THE CREATIVE ESSENCE OF LIFE

We think we know our bodies. After all, we've each lived in one for twenty, forty, eighty years. But just because we live in a thing doesn't mean we know a thing.

I lived in a house for the first twenty years of my life. Twenty years straight. I knew nothing of the construction, the electrical work or the foundation. In reality, I've lived in a house nearly every day of my life, but if I'm willing to be honest, deeply honest, I hardly know what makes a house at all. I know only the surface, the appearance, nothing of the inner workings.

Spirituality is a willingness to embody this level of honesty. Because our knowledge of the world and of the body is similar to the knowledge of a house. It's mostly the outer layers. It's mostly paint and walls. It's not the deeper reality. It's not the deeper *miracle* happening beneath it all. And a miracle is closer to the truth.

Any of us can logically agree with this. How worlds get built and stars lit and how the wheel of death gets turned to life is a great miracle. But we think this miracle lies elsewhere, at some unreachable distance. We think we can't touch it or come to know it right *here* because it isn't here. It only happens someplace else or perhaps over the course of millions and billions of years.

But have you watched this? You eat a handful of grapes in the morning and by the evening your body has turned them into a human being. Is this not that miracle?

Perhaps it's smaller. Perhaps it's a different expression, one that's lost its charm. But is it not that same creative event? If we took a graham cracker, stuffed it into a toaster and out came an iPad, most of us would need therapy. Yet every second, our bodies are doing even more and we don't bat an eye.

This is a miraculous unfolding. And it's happening within us each moment. If we have the devotion to begin resting beneath the surface of life, this energy can become clearer and clearer.

I'm not saying that this will set our lives ablaze. I'm not saying when we know this that it will always be out front before our eyes and in the forefront of our minds. It surely won't be. When we're in touch with this, we don't go around all day thinking, 'My body is a miracle, this food is a miracle, this tea is a miracle.'

But just imagine if you had your finger lightly on the pulse of this. Imagine if you carried a drop of awareness of the source behind the life process—the entire life process, within you and in the world. Imagine you when you know that which turns food into human beings and transforms death to life.

Again, it takes wading through the initial discomfort of dropping the old mind to truly *feel* this. Because the more mind-oriented a person, the greater the fog. If we are mind-oriented, there is no mystery, no novelty, no light.

By 'mind-oriented' I simply mean that our baseline is this; before the world reaches us, it's filtered through thoughts—it's not experienced directly, it's labeled and thought about. The result is our thought-worlds become more convincing than the actual world; our thought life more convincing than our actual *life.*

This is what's happening in society today. Right now, most of us only live in our minds. Which is to say we set up camp in seven percent of the body—only the head. Unless an aching pain or discomfort enters our awareness, we're so involved with all our mental happenings that we often feel a great chasm separating us from our bodies and our bodies from the world. Most of life's problems arise from this split.

MIND ENERGY OR BEINGNESS?

Once, there was a blind beggar holding up a sign: 'PLEASE HELP! Need water!'

The beggar was an old man, nearly skin and bones, so naturally many well-wishers came and placed cups at his feet. There were all different kinds—bowls, glasses, tin cans. All filled with water. After a few weeks, the beggar was surrounded by so much water no one could bring him more—yet he still wouldn't drink.

One day, a young girl approached.

'Excuse me,' said the girl. 'I've seen you sitting here for weeks begging for water. Why don't you take any of these cups?'

'It's simple,' replied the beggar. 'If I pick up a cup, then I'd have to put down my sign.'

'Yes, but then you could have as many cups as you needed.'

'But I don't need cups. I need water!'

. . . .

When we look out into the world as only a mind we're often like a blind beggar. We're looking for water in a world of cups.

We're so hypnotized by the names, roles and appearances of ourselves, our family members and the world that we miss the inner contents all together.

This is one of the greatest tragedies. In seeing every moment of our lives from only the mind—from *only* this physical body—we're blind to our likeness in others. We never glimpse our deepest Self in the world. We never see that all the different pots of life—all races, genders and clans; all fish and birds, dogs and cats—are drawn from the one clay. They are all made of the same earth energy. And deeper within, they are all the same waters—the waters of *beingness,* of *consciousness.* And it's only water that gives life.

Because have you noticed the qualities of water? Wherever water is, its essence is timeless and one. Place it in a pot, it fills the form of the pot. Into a glass, it fills the form of the glass. Wherever it is, it's always one whole. You cannot tell where one molecule starts and the other begins. And its essence is unchanging. Its form changes. Its shape and self-expression vary. But whether it's flowing or misting or solidifying, the water essence, the H_2O essence, is unphased. Thus, it's perfectly, naturally in tune with life. It's a great example of harmonious presence, of our deepest *being.*

The difference between water and the human family is most of us don't see our similar quality. We're blind to the *living water.* We don't see an inner dimension that is peaceful, whole and unchanging. Because right now, we're largely compartmentalized. We're preoccupied with only one cup—the cup of the mind. All the movements and sloshings and grumblings of the mind are where we live, where we give our attention. Naturally, tension arises. Particularly so because the cup of the mind is where all the self-doubts, limitations, regrets, traumas and lack are stored. And the more convinced we are by this cup, the more its stories and traumas start polluting the whole body. We can see it quite visibly.

Thoughts are always showing up in the body. Everyone over the age of twelve knows that a sexual thought influences their physical state, their emotional state. But so do all the others.

Think a few depressing thoughts and you start using the body in a depressing way. Your form becomes slouched, crooked and bent. A sense of weight and resistance is felt in each movement. Think a few restless thoughts and the same thing happens—the body becomes restless. You start using it in a jerky, erratic and mechanical way. This applies for all thoughts, for angry thoughts and unworthy thoughts and all the others—they become our body, our energy.

If all we know of ourselves is the seven percent of the mind, this becomes a great problem. Because the mind lives in a state of reaction. It only sees a world of cups and the cups are always changing, always bumping into each other. So the mind is always weaving some new gripe or offense or story of misfortunate. How many of these are happening within one day, within one hour?

All of these mental reactions place us on shifting sand. They're a dangerous foundation. They don't just influence the way we inhabit our bodies, they become the way we live our lives. Our bodies become molded and formed by our reactions—by depression, restlessness and irritability. Naturally, we start feeling hopelessness. We start feeling like a victim with little agency—agency over our mental state, our emotional state or the state of our lives.

This isn't to disregard deeper issues within one's body or life-situation. A person may be clinically depressed. A body may have hormonal issues, chemical imbalances. A mind may have a traumatic childhood or PTSD. These are unique situations. They often require external help. But even here, there's some agency. Where there's awareness there's always agency.

With awareness, what we do with our mental reactions is our choice. What we do with our body is our choosing. But without awareness, without a deeper sense of *being*, the choice feels fantastical. It appears not to be there. And if the choice isn't there, over time, our bodies take the shape of our reactions. They take the form of depression, of regret or irritability and harden into them.

This hardening turns into an even deeper depression. It becomes the baseline. What we're left with is a body that perpetually expresses what we don't want to feel. Soon, the deeper waters, the deeper *beingness,* is forgotten. And the more we remain locked in the cup of the mind, the harder it is to see.

. . . .

Traditionally, the movements of yoga are meant for awakening us to the inner water.

Such movements are beautiful. They can soften the outer edges, cleanse the flow of energy and invite the mind to return to presence. But the movements are not the only path. To inhabit and feel our *inner being* is the natural state. It's how a newborn experiences herself.

A newborn doesn't know she has a body. Her knowledge of herself is simply her knowing of this moment. This moment in its entirety. She has no context that she is anything but the buzzing lights, the doctor's hands and her mother's embrace. She is like water prior to the realization it has a cup. She feels no limitation. She feels herself as a borderless happening, a field of aware presence. Presence so clean and true that, like water, it is totally at one not just with itself, but also the world.

Learning how to use our bodies and minds is necessary. But returning home to the original state of *being* is the spiritual aim.

To do so, we don't simply feel the body. We don't become aware of the outer edges and borders of ourselves. The body actually gets *dropped* from consciousness. The outer body, its shape and appearance, leave your mind more and more, much like the body of a dancer in a dance.

At first, the dance she's learning is very mental. It requires a lot of thinking about herself *as* a dancer; how to be positioned, what to do with her legs, her feet, her arms. But as her dancing matures, all of these get dropped. She forgets about this particular movement and the next. She simply dances. She simply becomes the dance, the movements, the artform.

It's the same for a human being. We are born into a body and learn how to use it. We learn to eat and crawl and walk and run and so on. But after learning the instrument, the body is to be dropped, dropped from the mind, from the heart. It is to be the vehicle—not the 'I'.

So we don't feel the outer body. We drop our labels and relax *through* the body, *through* the cup. We turn into our constant, enduring quality—the inner space of the water itself.

There, we find a free field of energy or open field of presence. For water, we call this its true nature. For ourselves, we can call this space *being*.

DIVING INTO THE INNER WATER

We each as individuals must rally the courage and devotion to go beyond the veil of personhood—to wade beneath the borders of our mental energy and into the greater depths of our *being*. A simple practice can help us to start feeling the difference between the two.

As you're reading, become aware of your body. However you may be sitting and wherever you are, simply turn awareness onto the energy field of the body. If you can, drop your labels about it.

Don't think, 'Here is my body. Here is my foot. Here is my leg.' For a moment, just relax into what's there, what's nakedly there. No labels, no descriptions. Just the energy, just the vibration.

When relaxed and settled, ask: 'Do I know for sure my left foot exists?'

Drop the label 'left foot' and the label 'body' again. Take a moment to pause and start exploring with your eyes closed: 'Without looking and without labeling, do I know for sure my left foot exists?'

. . . .

It's a silly question. The mind will want to throw it out. But one of the most transformative steps of the spiritual journey, as well as our journey towards peace, contentedness and love, is knowing the difference between mental energy and beingness; which is the dimension of doing versus the dimension of being.

This question offers a small taste, an initial drop of clarity. So just for a moment, be willing to ask.

Direct awareness down within the inner space of the left foot. Don't give way to an old thought or memory. Simply open up and explore the sensation of *this* moment.

This is an important moment. See if you can catch a glimpse of the difference between mental energy and beingness. Sense the heat, the aliveness of the inner foot. Wade into the silent vibration, the pulse. Without moving, labeling or looking can you know for sure it's there? Can you feel the difference between mind energy and *being?*

· · · ·

There's no right or wrong answer. The question is simply a device. It's just a way of experiencing a part of the body in a fresh way, free of the mind, free of the seven-percent.

Because when we truly dive inward and explore the left foot, we don't feel so much what the mind tells us is there. We don't feel the outline of heel, sole, big toe, middle toes and so on. If we do, the mental image is still being held. We're still locked in our seven percent.

If we were speaking only to the knowing and feeling of this moment, this moment *cleanly,* we would likely describe the foot as a field of sensitivity. We'd likely say it's a vibrating presence or a warm, silent glow. Again, this is nothing transcendental. Initially, the mind will find it utterly mundane. But stick with it.

If you're still sensing the foot as *only* a rigid, separate object, erase the white board again. Clear the mental image. Relax deeper.

Feel the vibrating, the pulsing. If your foot is resting on the carpet, can you separate the feeling 'foot' from the feeling 'carpet'? What is the distance between them? Can you separate the two—one, a feeling that is 'foot' and the other, a feeling that is 'carpet' or 'hardwood' or 'bed'? Or is the sensation more seamless, uninterrupted? Is it more just an open field of warmth and presence?

This is just a small exercise. We can keep asking it right now or throughout the day or as the body and mind are drifting off to sleep in the evening. But we're not meant to continually cling to it, to keep asking over and over, 'Is my foot there? Is my hand there?'

Asking for the foot or for another part of the body is just a way of getting an initial taste. The true aim of the question isn't if we know whether something is there or not. The true aim is to glimpse the difference between what is mind energy and what is *beingness*.

Once an initial glimpse is there, then the deeper practice is available. Once the glimpse is there, then we drop the question and simply rest in the depths, explore the depths.

Perhaps we explore with awareness in the foot. This creates a sense of relaxed stillness. And the more light we shine on the *beingness* of the foot, the more light we shine on *beingness* as a whole. What it is, how it's distinct from mind becomes clearer. And the presence we feel in the foot is only one expression. It's a small drop of the inner waters of *being*. Resting awareness there is just like feeling the water in another cup. It's not the water of the mind, the mind energy. The mind energy is active. It's like the surface of the ocean. It tosses and waves. The water in the foot, in the hand is more subtle, but it's there. It's more a constant, deep stillness, so it's easier to miss, it's easier to overlook. But even it's only a stepping stone. Because if we're able to make the distinction—what is mind energy and what is *beingness;* what is thinking and doing and what is *presence*—then we can go beyond the foot. We can drop attention out of the foot or the hand or wherever and begin wading into the *beingness* of the heart. We can invite all of the separate cups—the feet, the hands, the legs, the chest—into one stream.

Resting in these waters is where the deeper stillness lies. It's similar to how practitioners feel after yoga. After the body is pliable, flexible and relaxed. It's similar to how a jogger feels after jogging—free and light—or how we may feel after a glass or two of wine. There's a sense of expansion and settled presence. There's a subtle self-forgetfulness and ease. All of these—yoga, exercise, alcohol and substances—are all means of drawing out these deeper qualities of *being.* The qualities that rest beneath the outer edges of our personality and programming, our patterns of thinking and reacting. We know we're approaching these when our state starts mirroring those of the above. When just by collapsing inward, relaxing inward, we start feeling as if we've just done yoga, returned from a jog or had a drink. We feel at home.

In fact, it's for this reason that yoga, exercise, alcohol and substances call to us—they're the closest to 'home' that most know how to get.

Meditation is being healthy about it. It's simply going home consciously. And the spiritual life stays there, stays in the ease, in the settled presence. It lives in the stillness of *being*, the 'stillness through which God is known'.

So we're simply learning how to go there without the help, without stopping to ask for directions or needing some other inputs—and without the blunted clarity that comes from using substances.

This experience isn't existential—a sense of ease or stillness isn't 'the *Self*'. But it's the initial fragrance of the dawning of presence.

CHOOSING PRESENCE

The thinking mind may go on insisting this is a fairy tale. After all, this isn't exactly tangible or practical. This isn't exactly for 'real life.'

We may know our *inner being*, but if we tumble down a flight of stairs, our body still bruises. If we get in an accident, it's still bound to hurt. If we know the inner waters, we'll still be going around bumping into other cups.

This is simply the nature of having a body, of having a cup. The cup is subject to breakdowns, to damages and change. So yes, the reality of the body still exists. There's no transcending or denying it. By moving from our depth of *being,* we aren't trying to change this reality. By moving from our depth of *being,* we're transforming our experience of it. We're transforming ourselves.

Because the body will break down, but what would it mean knowing the deepest you is beyond it? What would it mean to stop feeling yourself as a small subject in a world of endless things, one that will age and break and get sick and die, and to start knowing yourself as an abiding presence?

Imagine the difference in how you would experience yourself. Imagine your relationships when you start relating from presence as presence to presence—which is from wholeness as wholeness to wholeness.

As with fixing the mind on our breath, it takes initial effort. The hardest moments of wading into the ocean are getting through the early waves. So there is some effort needed. Especially because we've built up the muscle memory for mind energy. Wrestling with the mental waves has become the baseline. So each time we dive into deeper waters, the mind energy follows. Quickly, it yanks us back to the surface, to the body and the world. How could we start moving and living from the ocean, from *beingness?*

· · · ·

Once, an Olympic athlete was asked how he kept setting new records, how, despite the odds, he was able to keep making the impossible possible. He simply replied, 'By doing it.'

Accomplishing great things is simple. It's just doing it. It's just starting and continuing with a fire at its back. A fire of devotion, a fire of dedication and commitment. With doing and fire, we can rise above most things. We can become most things, even impossible things.

So how to do it?

Be devoted. Thirst for it. Learn your unique way of desiring after it. This is true for all meditative and spiritual paths. Then go the simplest way forward.

Don't get caught in the maze of trying to outrun the mind—trying to shoo away and outwit all the mental noise. That's all part of the drama, it's all more waves. It takes us deeper and deeper into mind energy.

Instead, just observe. Just feel the difference, the difference between being a mind and being presence. The difference between mind energy and *beingness*. Simply look to understand.

Each time you find yourself swept away in the mind, having run off to some other place, don't reject the place. Don't avoid or try to change or hate the place and the thought. Simply ask, 'Is this mind energy? Or *beingness?*' 'Does this story belong to thought or *presence?*'

This can quickly bring great clarity. Clarity because confusion is a quality of the mind, a movement in the mind. When we're confused, it means we've gotten lost amongst the waves of mind energy. Confusion, worry, restlessness, anxiety, anger—all of these take flight through mind energy.

So exploring this question offers great possibility. It organizes the wild nuances and complexities of the mind. They all start falling under the same filing system, under the same label; mind. Thoughts of work; mind. Thoughts of lunch and vacation; mind. Thoughts of regret and worry, anxiety and fear; mind.

It creates a great simplicity. Your mind itself becomes simple. Because there's no tangled web of conceptualizing or intellectualizing. There's no forgetting or searching for an old experience or trying to arrive at some non-existent pot at the end of the rainbow of thought. There's only *being* and, when a wave rises, the question—mind energy or *beingness?* Mind energy or *beingness?*

Mind energy is movement; *beingness* is still. Mind energy is complex; *beingness* is simple, child-like.

. . . .

As we do this, we'll see that some movements of the mind *do* require exploration. As we rest with the breath, *beingness* or any other meditation, we'll encounter this.

Some thoughts will ask for the light of awareness, the light of healing. And until they're given it, they keep popping up. They're wounds that need mending. They often need attention because we have so much rejecting energy towards them, years and decades of rejecting energy. So they require a more warm-hearted mind, a more welcoming mind. A mind that doesn't collapse out of, but wades into the wave of unresolved fears and traumas—directly.

These are our deepest, unconscious mental loops. They're our most consistent themes of fear and desire that overlay our depth of being.

So there are needed moments of exploration. There are moments of self-healing, mind and energy healing. It's part of the journey of coming *home*. It can be helpful to have a teacher or therapist or conscious community by our side to share their light, their perspective.

But the more we know *beingness,* the more truth comes about on its own. When to explore a thought and when to simply fall Self-ward starts shining its own light. This is the gift of simplicity and awareness.

So asking this question alone for ten minutes a day—mind energy or *beingness?*—can stoke the greater fires of transformation. Because who do the dramas and anxieties belong to in the end—*beingness* or the mind energy? Who do the anger, the worry and the fear look to for their existence—*presence* or thinking?

We each must see for ourselves.

INNER BODY PRACTICE

Paul had a problem. By the time he finished a third cup of coffee, he knew caffeine wasn't the answer.

He was always anxious in waiting rooms. There was something about the glaring lights and the smell of ammonia. It didn't help that he'd been waiting on test results for an hour.

'Why haven't they said anyth——?'

before his mind could stalk the wrong answer, he scanned the room for a distraction. Feeling the still warm cup between his hands, he placed his attention there. The cup was vibrant, almost soothing.

Quickly, his mind raced back to the test results. But instead of feeding into the drama, he sank into his body and gave himself over to the warm pulse of his hands. His breath deepened. His attention grew purer. And as he closed his eyes, a shift started happening.

At first, it was fragile and faint. His mind stayed in step with his surroundings—buzzing and antsy. Yet, the deeper he waded out of thinking and into *feeling*, the more he sensed the warm glow in his hands spreading. It expanded from the tips of his fingers to his open palms. His grip slowly softened. Free of tension, the glow grew purer, more inviting. And the more he felt into it, the more it opened, showering from palms to wrists, wrists to forearms, forearms to shoulders.

Briefly, his mind tried to rope him in again, to persuade him back into worrying. But Paul simply sat in the stillness and instead, turned more inward towards the peace. Gradually, his mind grew quiet, empty.

While the waiting room buzzed and beckoned, Paul gave way to a different reality. He began sensing a vivid aliveness emanating within his body.

This aliveness wasn't felt as a byproduct of the warm glow of the coffee cup, but the warmth seemed to invite his mind inward, like opening the blinds to the morning light. The light was always there, just thinly veiled. The more he relaxed, the more it washed over him.

With eyes closed, Paul started exploring this sense of *presence*, searching for its source and edges, its origins and ends. But as Paul sank more deeply into his body, just as before, the aliveness began spreading wider, purer; shoulders to chest, chest to stomach and stomach to legs. His whole body softened and soothed.

Resting in a deeper, more settled reality, a great insight arose. Suddenly, Paul saw his anxiety wasn't *in* the waiting room, not really. It wasn't actually in this moment or situation, not even in the glaring lights or smell—it was in him. It was simply what he was doing with it, what he'd *always unconsciously* been doing with it. It was simply his interpretation, his beliefs, his mind. And the deeper he waded into his body, the more he sank into the *presence* beneath it.

Soon, the aliveness grew so total that Paul felt his whole body as one seamless glow. This glow was expansive, all-inclusive. It was not divided between feet and calf, knee and thigh, shoulder and neck. Nor was it divided between his own body and the room. With eyes closed, there was only one glowing sense of presence, of *being*.

His mind raced to different matters—the endless 'what if's' of worry and concern. He thought to give in, but something made him pause. For the first time in Paul's life, he felt a deep clarity, a deep light go on.

All of these thoughts—questioning, worrying, projecting and fearing—were all different, yet they had the same feel. They were each unique. Like passing waves, they had their own shape, expression and story. But they were all in the same place, all different waves on the surface. Resting in deeper waters, they looked like faint ripples. Slowly, a clear distinction, a clear space between the waves of thought and the stillness of *being* started to appear.

He centered here, sensing that this experience of presence—of *being*—was actually the experience of himself, his *truest*, forgotten self. It was always here, always *him*. It was the silent quality of his life. A hush fell over him and the radiant glow of peace flooded his awareness. It washed over him so deeply, thought couldn't hope to pull him out.

After some time had passed, Paul was stirred by a voice.

'Sir,' the voice whispered, the owner laying a hand on his shoulder. 'We've got the results.'

Paul opened his eyes and smiled. Setting the coffee cup down, he was ready to meet what awaited.

DIRECTLY HOME

5 COMING HOME THROUGH THE MIND

Once, there was a captain and a blind first mate. Though the first mate was limited, he was a great help. He could clean the boat, hoist the sails, tidy up the captain's quarters and prepare meals.

One afternoon, the captain thought he'd enjoy a quick drink. Being a responsible seafarer, he decided the blind first mate should drive. The captain guided him up to the helm and placed the first mate's hands on the wheel.

'You got nothing but clear skies and open seas,' said the captain, tapping on the compass. 'Stay true!'

The captain scurried below deck. By his second drink, the sea had grown rocky. By his fifth, the ship was taking on water. Coming to his senses, he stumbled up to the deck.

The skies were black with rain and the waves the size of mountains.

'Keep true!' shouted the captain.

To the west of the boat, a massive wave swelled. The captain shut his eyes, bracing for impact. Just then, the blind first mate flung the mast to port side, somehow narrowly missing the wave.

'I said keep *true*!' Shouted the captain. A second wave swelled to the east. The first mate flung the mast starboard, narrowly missing their death once again.

'Aww, what do I know!' said the captain. 'You do you!'

Just then, a third wave surged in front of the tiny ship. The first mate flung the mast right, then left, then back right, narrowly avoiding their doom. Soon, the clouds began to part and the waves died down.

'Bloody hell, mate!' Shouted the captain after his blind helper. 'How can you steer when you can't even see?' But the first mate was silent.

'I said how can you steer when you can't even—' the captain froze, looking at the compass. The blind first mate had sailed 300 miles in the wrong direction.

'I thought I said keep true!' shouted the captain.

The blind first mate turned to the captain, then back to the mast.

'Am I driving?'

. . . .

The mind is a great helper. But use it for everything and we never get far.

It's easy to enter meditation or read books like this and wonder, 'Why do we have to be so against the mind? Aren't thoughts helpful? Isn't thought a sign of intelligence?' In fact, I once had a young woman come to me saying, 'I'm horribly insecure. But your approach doesn't work for me. I don't struggle with my thoughts.'

Feeling this way isn't uncommon. But how do we know we're insecure unless we're referring to our thoughts?

Perhaps we have a sensation, a feeling. A feeling we label as insecurity. But a feeling isn't insecure. A feeling is a feeling. It's just a sensation in the body. Remove the story *about* the feeling of insecurity—all the past memory and mind energy it rustles up—and it's actually quite close to the feeling of excitement and arousal.

So wrestling with insecurity, anxiety and low self-esteem in many ways is wrestling with our thoughts. It's less us responding to life, responding to the moment as it is, more us responding to ourselves, to what our thoughts would have us believe *about* the moment.

This is why two people turn one event into two realities— because no two minds are alike. For one person, slipping and falling gives way to laughter. It's a great comedy. And for another, it creates a deep sense of embarrassment. And still, for another, anger and another, apathy. The reality is the same—falling—but the creative experience is different.

INTELLIGENCE VERSUS INTELLECT

Our thoughts are always creating our reality. In fact, that's what thinking is—an act of creating, a vehicle for creating. It's what creates the possibility for something new to manifest, something unique and expressive. And no family is greater at self-expression than the human family.

All the modern comforts, technologies, industries, nations and social structures that exist today are the expressions of thought. They started as ideas. Language was an idea, tribes were an idea, the wheel was an idea, agriculture was an idea and trains, cars and cell phones were all ideas. They each arose within the mind and then appeared in the world.

This isn't just happening on the collective scale, on the historic scale, it's happening moment by moment in each of us.

You feel a pang of hunger—a gnawing flame in the gut. A thought of pizza arises. Thirty minutes later, a pizza shows up at your door. Hunger was there. The hunger is bodily, physical—it stirred a mental action. But thought created the next meal.

Thought is always actively creating for you. It's creating your surroundings—the art that covers your walls and the photos that fill your home. It's creating your relationships—what kind of people you attract and what you find attractive. And it's creating your house, your job, your lifestyle, your beliefs, your mood, your attitude and your sense of self. All of these trace their origin back to thoughts.

So thinking is the act of creating, creating what appears on the inner screen—beliefs, perspectives and feelings—and the outer screen—the world and your life situation. It's a wonderful tool. But it's not always intelligence. Intelligence is only that which works for you, not against you.

. . . .

Ernest Hemingway said, 'Happiness in intelligent people is the rarest thing I know.'

He speaks of the intelligence of thought, of the ability to think and retain and project and articulate. But is this *true* intelligence? If what we call 'intelligence' is making us unhealthy, is that intelligent? If what we call 'intelligence' is walling us off from life, raising our blood pressure, wrecking our relationships, driving us into sleepless nights and a life of poor health and compulsion, is that intelligence?

There's a story—once, a Christian, a Muslim and an atheist got into a gun fight. They each received fatal wounds and soon found themselves standing at the gates of heaven. There, God approached. 'You've all believed different tales,' He said. 'But each of you made such a misery out of life! And now you've died at each other's hands? How could this happen?' They turned to one another and shrugged, 'Intelligence?'

Intelligence is designed to move towards well-being, towards higher and higher states of well-being for the individual and the collective. If intelligence is creating unhealthiness in Hemingway, you or anybody, is that *real* intelligence?

After all, if someone is truly intelligent, why not make themselves happier and happier? Why not use their intelligence for them? Instead, those who claim the crown 'intelligent' are often found in the spring of life, their wallet is full, the sun is out and the sky is calling and they're too locked in their mental stall to enjoy it.

This is not intelligence—this is intellect. This is the result of thoughts having taken the wheel; of having an unconscious mind that keeps running, running, running. We're bound to arrive at misery. Whatever is perpetually running always lands there.

You love racquetball. You get to play every Sunday. This is a great joy. But you love racquetball and we lock you in a room. We force you to play all hours of the day. How quickly you'd hate it! How quickly joy would turn to misery.

So it is for all things—jogging, sleeping, reading, kissing your lover, going to the movies, sipping your cup of tea. If it's always happening, you're bound to want out. And even more so when it's always churning within you, when it's always stirring up the waters from inside out.

Many of us turn to our thoughts—the very source of the tension—to correct the tension. We try using mind energy to figure out where we went wrong, how we got here and to strategize a way out. There's nothing wrong with applying the mind in this way. There are times when the creative and analytic process is needed. For many daily tasks and for deeper unresolved traumas, it's a useful approach. But the misery of overthinking itself does not resolve through more thinking.

In fact, have you noticed this? Often, the more you think, the less resolved you feel. And the less resolved you feel, the more you think.

If we become a little inwardly conscious, we see that in our larger seasons of sadness or dis-ease, thinking is at its peak. Thought has unknowingly taken the wheel. But in our seasons of ease, of inner resolution, we find ourselves thinking less and less. And when we touch a moment of total resolution, total at-ease-ment—when we are hungry and we get the cake or lonely and we get the lover—we discover there's hardly a thought at all. The mind isn't adding any noise to the moment. Thought is simply silent.

This state of silence is what all the thinking is working towards. When we use the mind to try to strategize our way out of unwanted states, where we're actually trying to go is a state of inner silence, a state where the mind can be empty and we can simply *be*.

This is why it's said, 'Real thinkers don't think.' If you're truly intelligent, if you *truly* think and follow thought all the way down the rabbit hole, thought runs out. You start discovering the presence, the well-being and *love* that arise in its absence. And a lack of love is the only reason people are sick and unhappy—because love is well-being. Love is the highest state of well-being. Love is the highest understanding the mind can attain.

By 'love' I don't mean a feeling. I don't mean an emotion or an action. By love, I mean a certain vibration. By love, I mean a place you start living in, a place you start looking and creating from. Naturally, the more intelligent you are, the more you stumble inward into this place, into the love from which you never recover.

THE EYE OF THE STORM

The mind may say, 'I see how always thinking creates unhappiness. I see how an overactive mind is a problem. That's nice, but I'm still no closer to stopping it.'

This is perfectly natural. A man wandering in the desert is bound to be hungry. He's bound to carry a deep hunger if he's gone for days and weeks without food. But knowing his empty stomach is painful doesn't end the pain. It takes something more substantial, something more life-giving.

In the same way that empty stomachs growl, worldly minds overthink. They're both products of the same problem. Just as the empty stomach is growling out of lack, the worldly mind, the materialistic mind is also.

This is why things like 'law of attraction' and positive thinking rarely work. It isn't because thoughts aren't creating our future. It isn't because thought isn't turning ideas into objects and the non-physical into the physical. It's because it's tough to flow consistent energy towards being full when you're starving. It's tough to imagine being filled by the pizza or the fish when you're wandering in the desert.

So even if you dabble in such methods, even if you see thought is a tool for creating the future, you end up thinking as many thoughts about not having what you want as having it. Naturally, life serves up a bit of both. And until you can maintain a steady flow of energy in one direction, both will keep flowing your way.

It takes touching the deeper roots, the deeper ground of *being* for energy to start going where you want.

· · · ·

Imagine you are looking down on a hurricane—vast and violent. Its winds are ripping trees from the earth and ships from the sea. It's easy to get lost in the drama and the chaos; the endless twisting and turning. And if you get wrapped up in the winds, naturally you'll start feeling unsettled. The wind's nature is to go round and round, back and forth, on and on and on. But if you give all your attention to the wind, you'll be missing the hurricane's hidden quality. Because at its center, at the point which never changes, it is utterly tranquil, unmoving. It is completely drama-less.

We are each like a hurricane. We have intense activity, intense winds of desire and trauma on the surface. The more we live turned towards them, the more we confuse ourselves for the frenzy. The tossing and turning and whipping and raging. Naturally, we get little say in our state.

But if you're like a hurricane, you also have a silent center. It isn't found by running towards the wind, but by turning the mind around and wading into its source.

Peace is the intrinsic quality of depth. The more deeply you look at anything—the hurricane, the ocean, the human being, the atom—the more you find peace. In the depths of all cases, you uncover a place beyond form, movement and change. Which is to say, a place of silence, stillness, resolution.

This discovery brings great clarity. It can afford the freedom to direct your energies more continually upwards, more continually towards your choosing. Because only this reveals you are independent from the energies.

Only this shows that you are not a happy feeling or a sad feeling; you are not an anxious thought or a stoic thought. You are not the violent gust nor the easy breeze. You are that great potential which is capable of both.

You are that potential which can show up as weakness or strength. You are that potential which can give rise to compassion or contempt. You are that potential which can create technology and industry and cars and cell phones and peace and hate and abundance and warfare and everything in between.

This is what is meant in spiritual traditions saying you are emptiness, saying you are *sunyata*; nothing. It isn't a statement of belief—it's a level of perception, deep perception. It's not saying you aren't there. It doesn't mean you don't exist. It means you think yourself to be a good person, but you're not really a good person. You think yourself to be a bad person, but you're not really that either. So you are neither the relative good nor the relative bad. You are attributeless. You are that open space of creative potential.

Recognizing this is what relaxes the mind. When you find the place in you that's already resolved, that's already open and empty, the mind starts resolving itself. It starts becoming empty like the cup and open like the sky.

This isn't to say we *never* think again or that desire isn't there. That's a misunderstanding. Enlightenment, *Self*-realization, coming *home;* these don't forever *end* desire—they take the lack out of it. They transform it.

A starving man has a burning desire for food. Once he's had his fill, the desire for food is gone. But a new desire, a higher desire takes its place—a desire less for the body, more for the mind, for the heart.

In the same way, once *realized,* our desires shift. They start transforming from the physical to the spiritual; from lower to higher.

These desires are those for life, for unity, for beauty, for creation, for sharing, for possibility, for play, for God and for higher and higher states of being. These are the desires of the deeper 'I', of the creator. After all, any true creator would desire. Otherwise, why create? Any true buddha would desire. Otherwise, why *dharma*—why share *truth*?

A creator and a buddha simply have whole desires, godly desires. They desire like the flower desiring the sun, the moon desiring the sea and life desiring after life. These are the desires of love, of the vibration of love. It simply takes returning to the heart of things to start moving from them.

LIVING AS 'CHRIST'

Who am I? This whole book we've been exploring it. At this point, you can recite the answers; 'I'm not the body, I am the presence'; 'I am not the mind, I am *awareness, beingness.*'

But these words alone are just words, just mind energy. We can have all the words we want. We can have the words of Jesus or Buddha or Rumi or whoever in our mental library. But just because we have Jesus' words rolling around in our heads doesn't mean we're experiencing words the way Jesus did. Just because we have Buddha's ideas swirling in our minds doesn't mean we're any closer to realizing the nature of our mind. And this must happen for *true* transformation.

Imagine if every time you said 'I', you were referring to even the subtlest shade of Jesus's 'I', of Buddha's 'I'. Imagine if whenever you spoke or thought 'I', it implied even a little of the universal 'I' or God's 'I'. That's transformation. That's coming *home*. That's what is meant by 'living as Christ'. It doesn't mean we believe in Christ. Belief is only a first step. It's what gets us on our way. But belief is not a destination. Belief is like a boat—it helps us cross the river. It takes us to the shore of realization. But to realize, we must step out and experience. Otherwise, belief becomes another barrier, another attachment. And only by going beyond barriers and attachments do we begin 'living *as* Christ.'

What does this mean? What does it look like to start living *as* Christ? It means what it says it means—that each time we say 'I', we are referring to Christ. And each time we refer to Christ, we're referring to 'I'.

This may seem an impossible feat. And to the mind, it most certainly will be. Because the 'I' of Christ, the 'I' of buddha isn't the mind's 'I'. It doesn't have anything to do with mind energy at all. It's the inner depths, the *light of life* from which mind energy spills forth.

So the mind must wade more deeply inward than the 'I' of the body, the 'I' thought. That is what is meant by being silent—wade beneath the 'I' thought, beneath body-mind energy. Silence does not mean simply silence. It does not mean we try and try to quiet the body and the mind. It means we go inward, we wade into the silence.

It is like you are swimming in the ocean, bobbing in the waves. Someone says, 'Go to the silence.' They don't mean wrestle down the waves until they're no more. They mean wade down, down, down. Down to the still waters. That is what is meant by silence—to wade more deeply into your inner ocean, beneath the 'I' thought.

One of the ways we go there is by asking and becoming the question, 'Who am I?'

WAKING UP AS AWARENESS

Each morning your eyes open and the world appears—Who am I?

It's most useful to ask in the morning, before too much of the world gets in your mind, before the day takes your 'tabula rasa' away. So ask it in the morning.

You wake up, your eyes open and the world appears—who am I? You rest here for a moment. As the wakefulness becomes clearer, thoughts will begin writing on you; 'I need coffee, 'I need to get ready for work', 'I need to worry about so and so or this or that'.

But you leave the world alone. You simply relax into the question—'Who am I?'; 'To whom do these thoughts come?'—and wade back into your *beingness*.

It's helpful to do this in the morning, because as soon as mind energy starts rushing in, you seem to rush out. And mind energy is not so visible, so obvious. It's not so clearly and plainly written on top of you. It's subtle. It starts in ripples, not waves. And because it's so familiar, because you're so used to its company, you get swept off out of habit. You don't even realize when you've gone. You don't even realize when the rippling appears, if you start swimming outward, that they start taking you away from your *Self*.

With this inquiry, with 'Who am I?', we're throwing the process in reverse. We open our eyes in the morning, we rest in the *beingness*. We ask 'Who am I?' 'Who is this?' And when mind energy arises in the form of a problem or a title or a name, we draw it back to the source, to the heart region, the heart center. To me, that's where it is most powerful to ask the question: to the heart.

In the heart, you are no longer asking for some thought about reality, you are *feeling* for reality. You are no longer clinging to the mental walls that separate your being from the being of others, you are feeling into the one *being* beneath all forms.

So ask it and ask it early. It's easier to keep a fire burning than to rekindle it. Ask it before you lose yourself in the winds of thought. And when you ask, *feel* for it. Because the mind will say, 'There's no point in asking the question—I don't get any answer.' 'I keep asking 'Who am I?' but find nothing.'

Often, if we're asking with the mind, we'll feel this way. But every time we ask the question, truly ask, we get the answer. There's no way out of it. We ask the first time—we get the answer. We ask the thousandth time—the same answer. And the answer comes instantaneously, universally.

You turn inward; 'Who am I?' The instant you ask 'Who am I', there is utter silence. You ask again, 'Who am I?' That very instant, there is a blank, an open space. You've swung open the door, burst inside and discovered no one.

If you're asking with the mind and looking for an object, a thing, you say, 'I ask, but I find nothing'. If you're asking with the heart looking for a reality, you say 'I ask *and* I find nothing.'

The nothing, the silence, the openness, the spaciousness is the answer. It's your deepest *Self,* your *presence.* This is why asking 'Who am I?' and silence are the same thing. The question simply keeps you alert, receptive.

So sink into the heart and *feel* for it. Don't search for some object-answer. That would mean you still remain of the world. Drop the world. Become the question, become the openness. Who am I? Who am I? Who am I?

It will seem like no big deal at first. This is okay. A drought doesn't end at the first drop. More is needed to make a difference, to bring new life. So open the flood gates and ask each morning. Soon, you'll find yourself asking it throughout the day. It's the natural unfolding of *truly* asking the question—you start asking it, becoming it more and more. Your intention and honesty grow with greater and greater purity.

And if you're truly devoted, you'll see that unlike many other paths, you don't have to make time for this so much.

The other paths are often meditations *on* something. This is a question you enter into.

You can rest in the question while moving out into the world, while the body is doing its thing. The muscle memory and intelligence are capable of living your life just fine. Your input is rarely needed. You can rest undistracted in your own being, in the question more and more. And the more you're resting in the question, the more mind energy starts softening, which is your endless thoughts, complexities and conditionings. Slowly, awareness starts becoming clean. Your mind starts dropping knowledge. Knowledge about objects, about the world, about yourself. You still know these things, these relative things, but are not limited by them. That is why the path of self-inquiry is often called 'vedanta'; 'the end of knowledge'.

As knowledge starts falling away, you see there is little of which you are *absolutely* certain. Where the grasshopper or the sycamore tree or the universe comes from, why it is here, to what end it's moving—who is to say any of this? You've never known. And without borrowed knowledge, you start being honest with yourself. You start *seeing* the mystery.

And it is not just the outer world that is mysterious, but the inner world also. For the first time, you discover you no longer even know yourself. You see that truly calling yourself *awareness* or *being* is just as false as calling yourself 'Andrew' or 'Sarah'. Both are thoughts. Both are limitations.

For a worldly person, this is a great problem. Not knowing who you are creates a total break-down. You start questioning everything about you and your beliefs and your decisions and your free will and your place in the world.

This is why body and breath, meditations and mantras and different spiritual approaches exist. Because we're not all ready to go directly through the small 'I' and into the *beingness,* the void.

So for a person whose life is rooted in knowledge of the physical, of the changing, it can bring a great crisis. But for the meditative person—for the spiritual person—seeing you don't know who you are is *the* breakthrough. It creates the possibility of living *as* Christ, as Truth, as the whole.

This is why you ask the question—Who am I, Who am I, Who am I?

EMBRACING A NEW BEGINNING

For many, this direct questioning tastes like stale crackers. It seems completely bland and flavorless. It's just like turning the mind to the breath or the inner body. But the more meaningless it feels, the less likely we've asked the question. The less likely we've *really* ever asked it with a true longing. Not just a longing to prove our old mind right. But a longing for a direct encounter with *life.*

Find your longing. Find whatever helps you catch the fire. The fire can be one of curiosity or a need for truth. Or it can be a burning for joy or liberation from sorrow or God or whatever. But the longing must be true. It must create light. Only if it stirs a burning light in us will we open our hearts and drop our minds. Otherwise, we'll ask the question—who am I?—while trying to swim down, down, down into the silence, but we'll keep clinging to our life vest. The life vest of mind energy and knowledge. We'll try so hard to swim and swim into the silence, beneath the 'I' thought, beneath words and beliefs and knowledge, but the vest will keep dragging us back.

Don't let your knowledge of yourself keep you from yourself. Don't let your knowledge about scriptures and Christ and Buddha and whoever keep you from beginning to see the world as they saw it.

At least for five minutes a day in the morning, be willing to surrender your conclusions. Because as long as you keep holding to the old conclusions, you'll never truly ask the question. And your knowledge of yourself will remain entirely of the physical, of the relational.

You'll keep believing you are *just* Sarah, Andrew, John. You are a this or a that and you are this title or that title. But you won't see that all your names and titles are not for you—they're for others. 'Sarah, do this.' 'John, I love you.' 'Andrew, tell so-and-so dinner is ready.' You will never see that you actually have no name or title for yourself. To yourself, you are simply this aware knowing—just this *wakefulness,* just *I AM.* Everyone to themselves is just *I AM.*

If you wandered into the desert or the rainforest, this *I AM* would start crystallizing, just as Jesus' and Buddha's did. Or if you sat in a dark closet for a week or went somewhere away from society it would as well. You would see most of yourself is not *really* yourself and most of your problems are not really problems. Most of your problems are what society has conditioned you to think of as problems. You would see most problems don't even exist and you really have no name and no title.

Out in the forest, you would be Robert in relation to who? Alone with your Self, you would be an accountant or this or that in relation to what? Your whole experience of yourself would start falling away. You would start making room inside for all of nature, for all of existence.

. . . .

The more openly and intimately you ask 'Who am I?'—starting in the morning and then spontaneously throughout the day—the more this openness starts unfolding, gradually unfolding with increasing clarity. Eventually, with devotion, you start touching moments of taking deep sleep into the world, or in religious terms, you start living in the stillness through which God is known. It leaves you whole and increasingly holy. A wholeness and holiness more and more independent of circumstance.

When it's time for vacation, you are free, at ease. It's Monday, it's time for work, the same freedom, the same ease. You're sailing under open skies or rocking sleepy children, you are relaxed. You are reading of the hunger and poverty and unrest in the world, you are at peace.

You help. You do what is needed. You serve and raise the human family higher and higher through the role existence asks of you, but you don't pay with your peace, with your vibration of love. It is well with your soul.

This is true intelligence, true freedom—when it matters less and less what the world gives you.

Just sitting with this, you begin feeling freer.

MIND PRACTICE

'I can't do this anymore,' Amelia said, slamming her phone down. She glared over to an old family photo at the edge of her desk—a weekend getaway in the Bahamas—but found no relief.

She was tired of feeling angry. It didn't just rise and fall in passing waves. It seemed continual. It seemed to be gurgling up from a boiling pot that had no bottom. And despite going to therapy, reading books, joining a church and even taking antidepressants, she was still overflowing.

On a nearby shelf, a small book caught her eye. It was blue and small. She'd thumbed through it before—her mind could even conjure a few passages. Something about awareness and presence. But though the words seemed promising, the message felt dull. In *real* life, it seemed to offer no more relief than her family photo. Still, she felt a tugging, a calling to thumb through it again, if only for a distraction. But something inside stopped her. She paused, silently. And instead of turning to a book or a photo, a phone call or a cigarette, slumped into her office chair.

'Why am I *so* unhappy?'

She sat with the question. A thought of her boss appeared. They'd never had a particularly warm relationship. But lately, she'd begun to project this boiling onto him. Anytime she thought of him, her chest started rattling. Anytime he called, her mind caught flame. But as she sat quietly with the feeling, simply with the feeling, she couldn't shake the familiarity of it. The feeling wasn't just for her boss. It was the same feeling she'd blamed on traffic that morning and on her husband last week. It was even the same feeling she'd often had growing up with her mother.

'I....'

She felt a subtle shift. Her unhappiness always seemed complicated, brought on by long lines, traffic, people, deadlines and more. But as she sat with the feeling, she sensed its source was actually quite simple, quite obvious. While anger appeared to swallow her for many different reasons, the feeling itself was always the same—and it was always *hers*. Her feelings didn't belong to her boss. Her feelings didn't belong to her husband, her mother or her morning commute. Her feelings were *her* feelings. Slowly, she began sensing that perhaps she was responsible.

'Have I been making myself unhappy?' Amelia wondered, for the first time, turning away from the world and looking inward.

'*Who would do that?*'

Amelia examined her life; her influences, choices and roles. Soon, a thought of her job appeared. She'd been an accountant at Roper and Associates for nineteen years. She had a 15x15 office only three blocks from home and had settled into a nice life here. It was, in many ways, *her*—it suited her. It matched her character, her energy, her style. But she knew she hadn't *always* been here. *Before, I was a part-time clerk across town. And before that, a stay-at-home mom and before that, at college out of*—Suddenly, a car swerved behind her; a shiny green sedan, its red tail lights shimmering in the photo frame on her desk. She turned to face the image.

There, she could see herself smiling at 28; blonde, healthy and happy—at least relatively. She softened her gaze before catching her current reflection at 61, all baggy eyes and greying roots. Clearly, things had changed. She'd grown, she'd aged and in her aging, had become someone different, someone new. But deep down, beneath the wrinkles and wear, she knew she was still the same *her*. She was still Amelia, still her self. Who that self was, however, she wasn't sure.

'Everything about me is changing,' she closed her eyes. 'Yet, there's this *part* of me that's never changed. And it seems to keep making me unhappy, increasingly unhappy.'

She relaxed deeper… *What is it?*

A million thoughts began racing, personal thoughts. Thoughts that held a deep sense of intimacy, a deep sense of 'me'; the easy smiles of her young daughters and the bedroom of her childhood home; her mother's southern drawl and the mounting stress of her work-life. A few of them called to her, tugging her out of the moment. But she kept finding her way back. And once there, picked up the question once again; 'What is it? *Who am I?*'

She sat in silence as the afternoon passed, working at the question, not to be turned away. And each time a thought appeared—a thought of lunch or her boss or whatever—she'd steer the ship back on course, back to the question. And in simply asking, patiently asking, she realized something quite odd; even her thinking wasn't true. It wasn't *her*. Her thoughts were always washing in and washing out. One moment here, another there. One moment, her mind was full, the next, empty. But it never seemed to change *her.* She always was. And she didn't seem to become more herself while thinking or less while not. In fact, she felt quite the opposite. In the gaps between thinking—between all the drama and self-talk—she sensed something more true, more enduring. Slowly, a subtle realization washed over her:

'I'm not *just* my thoughts.'

Her breathing soothed. And with it, a faint sense of relief blossomed. She turned her attention towards it. There was an opening of the chest, a settling of the gut, an ease. But just as soon as it arrived, Amelia found it also leaving her. In its place, a familiar dread arose, washing over her body, washing into her mind. But she wasn't to be turned away. She didn't get overly involved or swim too far outward. She simply waited, watching and allowing. And in allowing, even the dread began to ripple out, to settle.

A new light went on, a new clarity; feelings weren't so different from thoughts. They were a tad more inward, a tad more personal. But just as flashing, just as momentary. She sat silent and alert. More alert than ever. And in that alertness, a subtle space appeared.

Amelia sat there—open and empty. She began searching, quietly searching to see if this space changed, to see if it was *her.* Yet, it seemed that it was out of this space that all of 'her' appeared—all of her thoughts and feelings, opinions and judgements, desires and beliefs. All of her mental and emotional energies. It seemed it was out of this empty, open space that all of her life had risen into being.

Suddenly, her whole body relaxed in a deep clarity, a deep trance. 'This space is what I am.'

The space had always been filled—thoughts were always washing over her, feelings always rising and falling—but when inwardly silent, inwardly still, she sensed a deeper constancy, a deeper, unwavering light. She couldn't shake the sense that this light, this peace, had always been with her, it had always *been* her. It was her enduring quality. It couldn't be separated, only overlooked. It couldn't be damaged, only forgotten. She sank into a new realization.

'This me isn't creating unhappiness... this me seems to be a sort of happiness itself.'

She sat silently, for the first time, feeling into her deeper *being*. And as she did, her mind kept chatting, unconvinced. It was buzzing with the same old thoughts; thoughts of deadlines and stress. Then thoughts of dinner and home and of all this silence being a mountainous waste of time. But for the first time, there was space around them, air underneath them. She waded deeper towards them, deeper *Self*-wards.

'I am simply this open awareness,' Her heart seemed to say. 'I'm not my roles... accountant, mother, wife; I'm *aware* of my roles. I'm not my thoughts... work, home, lunch, dinner; I'm *aware* of my thoughts. I'm not my moods... happy, sad, excited, stressed; I'm *aware* of my moods.'

I'm aware, I'm aware, I'm aware, Amelia said to herself.

'I am....'

She relaxed, realizing that this inner depth, this inner spaciousness couldn't be labeled. Even this label—'I am'—

wasn't truly *her*. It was her mind *thinking* about her. This aware presence, the enduring *her*, felt so open, so pure that it seemed closer to nothing at all. Her true *being* felt formless, dimensionless. But she sensed deeply, intuitively, that it was the same her she'd always been. It was the same her she'd been at fifty-three as at thirty-eight, at twenty five as seventeen. It never moved, altered or aged.

She opened her eyes and smiled, her gaze settling on the old family photo. She picked it up.

'If this spaciousness, this peace is in me, then it must be in everyone. What 'I am', my husband is, my children are... and even my mother and my boss. It must be the same 'I' for everyone, for all people of all races, cultures and backgrounds.'

She sunk more deeply inward, her eyes soaking in the sunlight that danced along the floorboards. Before, she couldn't shake the weight of unhappiness, decades of unhappiness. It had reconfigured her body, her face, her everything. But suddenly, in this moment, she couldn't untangle herself from peace, a peace that seemed to be her very truth, her very life—a peace she seemed to be looking out *from*.

She sat in a silent gaze, staring with renewed fondness, renewed love at the photo of her family. After a few moments, the phone rang. The screen lit up in bold, black letters; *BOSS*.

Gently, Amelia put down the photo, smiled and reached to answer.

DIRECTLY HOME

6 YOUR MAP OF AWAKENING

COMING *HOME* IS SIMPLE.

'Whatever you give attention to brings more of it.'

Don't overcomplicate coming home. The whole journey is a shift in attention.

Because have you noticed this? Whatever you give attention to brings more of it. A husband buys his wife a dozen yellow daisies—beautiful and vibrant. She goes about her normal day. Nothing is different, the world is the same. There's only one change; her mind is carrying around yellow daisies. And suddenly they start blooming everywhere. She starts seeing them on street corners and in front yards. She sees them on office desks and in grocery lines. As her attention of them is growing and growing, the more and more they're coming to her.

Or perhaps you have a new love interest. He or she drives a red Nissan Altima. Have you noticed this? Instantly, it's the most popular car on the street. You go to the grocery store, to the office, to the repair shop, it doesn't matter. You keep driving, more and more red Nissan Altimas keep arriving.

Whatever you give attention to brings more of it. If we give attention to all our mental energy, psychological dramas and old bag of problems, we'll get more of them. If we start self-emptying and giving attention to our depth of *being*, the same will happen. It will seem as if life is giving us more and more of it, more and more peace, more and more joy, more and more effortlessness. We must simply let go of what's failed to fill us so we can start giving attention to what does.

The mind may say, 'This is too boring. This is too simple. It can't work.' The mind says this as if it needs to be complicated.

It's precisely because it's simple, it's boring, that it offers a sense of liberation. Only something that's simple takes you back to having a simple mind, a mind that is ordinary and open and new. Only a simple mind can experience the spiritual, can touch oneness and timelessness. Only a simple mind can recover the wonder that there at the dawn of life.

So rouse yourself to enthusiasm. Shift attention off of the complex, the intricate, the world of ten thousand things. Start moving it towards the simple, the singular, the unchanging.

BEGINNING WITH HEART IS THE WAY

'The type of meditation is less important than the heart with which you enter it.'

After this clarity, generally the next question is, 'Okay, but which path do I take to the simple, the direct, the unchanging? Do I use the breath or the body?' Or 'Which is better; Self-inquiry or silence?'

Many of us wrestle with these questions for years. We wind up strategizing and overthinking and running back and forth from one meditation to the next and back again—all the while feeling that none of them *actually* work.

See now that this approach can't take us anywhere—it never gets started. It never *truly* gets started with the heart. Because even while meditating, the mind is chattering with one foot out the door. It's wondering about some other meditation. It's looking to some better way or different path. Naturally, this leaves us unfulfilled. We only seem capable of half-baked realizations—and never living embodiment.

It's better to just pick one and go. Go with all of you. When you're caught in the rain, you don't run in circles around the outside of the house. You don't stand there brooding over which is better: the front door or the backdoor. When you're caught in the rain, you simply go inside. You choose a door and go. It's the same with meditation. If you want out of the rains of frustration, loss and trauma, you have to go inside. Where else can you go? You have to pick one door and commit to using it, fully using it. And know that no matter which one you choose, they're all leading to the same house.

All the methods in this book and all the meditations and spiritual traditions the world has to offer are simply doors to the same house. They take you inside, into the one life, the one light. Don't worship the door or debate or argue over which is better. You can only do this from the outside looking in. When you enter, all these debates and arguments are dropped. Because the doors themselves are vastly secondary. *Home* is primary—shifting awareness, seeing through and as the *light of life* is primary.

So enter through whatever door is calling, whatever door feels most natural today. Try one for a month, two months. And along the way, take stock. Is it working for you? Not working for you as in, 'Are you getting bliss? Are you *realized?* Are you manifesting your dreams?' But is it working for you—are you seeing things more clearly? Are you taking more responsibility; responsibility for your thoughts, your moods, your life?

Let these be the initial bars of success. If after a month they aren't there, then follow your heart to another door. And if none of the doors in this book take, find a different way. Find your meditation, your door *home.*

Perhaps sitting still isn't for you at all. Perhaps you're more action oriented, energy oriented. Enter through the door of selfless service. If your heart is continually serving others, naturally the distance between you closes, your inner energy starts matching the outer energy. Seated meditation will help illuminate and center this. It'll ensure you have a less bumpy ride and a more thorough arrival. But either way, if the heart is in it, you'll sense a yoga, a loving disposition.

And if not selfless service, then perhaps the door of loving devotion. If you truly love and are devoted to God or an ideal or your family, community and friends, the same gift is yours.

So enter through whatever door works, whatever cracks your heart open. Simply enter through one and begin with a full heart, a worshipful heart. Beginning with heart is the way.

HOW TO ENSURE A DOOR OPENS FOR YOU

'Start letting go to the edge of your desire and any practice works.'

You get your deep driving desire. If your deep driving desire is for money, you shift attention towards money and you get it. If your deep driving desire is for power, you shift attention towards power and you get it. Perhaps it takes years, decades, but if it's true—if you *worship* it—it arrives. Some expression of it arrives.

What are you worshipping? What are you watering with your desire?

In the 1890's, John Rockefeller visited a Hindu monk. Rockefeller was very unhappy. He had the world, but it didn't ease the hunger, the need for more and more. But when he arrived, the monk was less than impressed. He didn't even greet the famed businessman who was entering his study. This lit a fire in Rockefeller. No one treated him this way. 'I am the wealthiest man in America!' He shouted. 'And who are you? You won't even address me?' But the monk was unmoved. He simply told Rockefeller that all his wealth would be better spent on the world than on himself. Of course, Rockefeller didn't stay to hear more. He quickly turned about face, leaving empty handed.

We can't know what Rockefeller *really* wanted. We can't know why he visited the monk. Perhaps simply unhappiness. Perhaps curiosity. But whatever it was, we know one thing—he didn't want it more than his pride. So naturally, whatever he came for he left without. His pride kept him from it.

What is keeping you from *home*? What is it you're *really* wanting?

It's been said, 'Where your heart is, there is your treasure, there is your life.' What are your thoughts telling you about your heart? Ask yourself, 'What sits at the top of the totem pole of my desires?' 'Where does the desire for spiritual freedom, for peace and truth sit?'

Don't pretend spiritual freedom is at the top when it isn't. This will only create frustration. Don't force spiritual freedom to the top when it's not. This will only create more

tension. Be honest. Be sincere. The sincere seeker finds—
'What do I desire above spiritual freedom, above coming
home?'

Make a list. However much is on it is fine. You can keep
them all for now. Just begin letting go of all that sits below
them. That's all that's needed today. Just begin renouncing
all the petty thoughts, conditionings and social norms that
you don't like anyway. Empty them from the pockets of
your mind. Renounce all that is less important, that isn't
serving the higher aim.

This is how you start, wherever you are. Whether you've
been a seeker or religious or non-religious or a staunch
materialist. It doesn't matter. We each have old thoughts
and conditionings we can shed. In fact, we each have
thoughts and conditionings we know we'd be happier
without.

So wherever you are, find your door, your meditation and in
the gaps of daily life, begin letting go to the edge of your
desire, renouncing to the edge of your desire. See what is on
your heart, where the desire for spiritual freedom is and let
go of all that's below it.

If you start taking it to the edge, surrendering thoughts to
the edge, each day, each week, it will start expanding. If you
let go of all that's below your desire for freedom and light,
you'll approach freedom and light. You'll begin *embodying* the
realization. Then the choice to desire further appears. The
desire purifies itself.

USING LIFE'S UPS AND DOWNS

'Can you in good times and bad times keep your heart one-pointed on the Ideal?'

The mind may say, 'This sounds great... but you don't understand. I have this problem and this issue and this past.' Or it says, 'Every time I think I'm ready for letting go, for spirituality, something pops up. Before I can realize the spiritual or find peace and happiness, first I must accomplish X, Y, Z.'

These are all simply ways of extending the timeline of suffering. The time to start is now. Know that all who now live in the peace and contentedness for which you're longing lived also in the hardship and pain you now call home. All is precisely as it needs to be for you to shift attention to the larger truth. All who are sitting under roofs with full stomachs and paid rent are beyond well-provisioned. The question is simply one of desire.

Is this something *you want*? Is it on your heart or not? Because in the end, whether we find ourselves in good times or bad times doesn't matter. If the desire is there, it doesn't matter. Bad times test our will. Good times test our devotion. Both are for our inner blossoming.

Can you in good times and bad times keep your heart one-pointed on the Ideal? For a person interested in spiritual freedom, that's the question, the metric: 'In good times and bad times is my awareness centered in the same truth, the same Ideal?' Or at least, 'In good times and bad times, is my mind increasingly resting in the Ideal—in meditativeness, in awareness, in God?'

This is a powerful question. If you start asking it, you'll stop being a problem maker and you'll start being a spiritual opportunist. All moods and life situations will offer you deeper waters. Because if in the waves of positive and negative energy your mind rests in the Ideal, the Ideal starts crystalizing. It becomes the central object, the central light. Soon, your thoughts and moods start orbiting around it.

This is how you 'become enlightened' or live fully-embodied in the *Self*—you begin one-pointedly resting your heart in them. And whether we like it or not, this will have to happen. Whether we like it or not, we have to make the timeless our constant companion.

First, we realize the light and then draw nearer and nearer to *being* it. But as our vision grows clearer, our desire grows cleaner. As we let go to the edge of our desire, it moves up the totem pole. It has no choice. The desire for freedom takes you to freedom. When true, the desire for spiritual freedom purifies itself. Because when you truly see what's keeping you from being free, you become less and less interested in what binds you. When you are no longer interested in what binds you, the pendulum of desire shifts. It swings away from the outer shackles of the world to spacious freedom; from material to spiritual; from you to *Self*, to God.

All the ups and downs of life are there for us to realize this.

MAKE YOUR HOME A DECLARATION OF YOUR VISION

'Bridge the gap between the physical and the formless in your environment.'

The journey to resting in inner silence or holding to one ideal may seem impossible. Hopefully, the first pages of this chapter offer a map. Still, there are ways to make the passage easier, ways to invite the mind into its *source* that are smarter, not harder.

One of those ways is physical. It's inviting the outer world into harmony with the inner ideal. It's bridging the gap between the physical and the formless.

You can start today. Ground your physical spaces with flowers of devotion. Find your highest representation of the *Self* or 'God' or divine love. Fill your life with its fragrance. Be aware of what others value and worship, but don't be influenced. How you see God depends on how you see. No two Buddhists have the same mental image of Buddha. No two Christians have the same mental image of God. God calls to one because he looks like compassion and another because he looks like strength. Still, others because he looks like a father and some because he appears as divine mercy. All hearts and minds have a unique thirst. Naturally, we're quenched by the highest water in unique ways.

What version calls to you? Whether you're religious or irreligious, what vision of the Absolute—or the highest ideal you can imagine—resonates most deeply?

This vision will not be the Absolute, obviously. 'God' cannot be held in a picture on the wall. But if it's the right picture, it can help draw Him out of you. Sit with an image of Jesus or Krishna or some sage or spiritual lover. You start to get a feel of what's behind their eyes. It starts calling it out of your own.

Who's image might be able to do this for you? It can be a person or a thing. But a person will be felt more personally, more deeply. A person will get your heart working, not just your head.

So who inspires you? Whose embodiment of *spirit* or compassion or love calls you to the same embodiment? Find that thing, that symbol, person or persons and get them in your eyes. Invite their fragrance into your life. Make them your companion. Place images of that which reminds you of your higher aim on your desk and the dash of your car. And don't stop at images. Listen to the sweetness of music that ushers your mind into the deeper waters. Read spiritual books and lectures that add to your desire and surround yourself with enlightened hearts. Fill up your senses with God. Make Him easy to find. This will keep you going when spiritual embodiment doesn't feel practical, when you don't know the way and along life's mountainous road of ups and downs.

AWAKENING A NEW EARTH: FOR YOU AND OTHERS

'The start of a new earth is in each of us each moment. No effort to spark it is in vain.'

This book isn't revelatory. In fact, it hasn't told you anything you don't already know.

You may have yet to swim in the depths of your own peace or glimpse the light of transcendent reality, but still you know all that's needed. You know that deep down you are not simply a storehouse of memories and food. Whether you have a Christian mind or a Buddhist mind or an agnostic or atheist mind, you know that there's a deeper dimension, a deeper reality to *you*. All it takes is following this knowing.

If you follow this knowing and your heart is in the following, then naturally everything in this book becomes yours. Naturally, what you deep down already know to be true becomes all-pervasively true. And if you choose that truth, if you worship it and love it and pour yourself upon it, it chooses you—*You* choose you, your deeper *being* chooses you, *God* chooses you.

In all practical aspects, nothing will change from this. Yes, you'll have more agency, more autonomy. You'll have more peace and more inner freedom. But on the surface, you'll still be your 'self'. If you're John Doe, you'll remain John

Doe. You'll keep having the body-mind of John Doe, the relationships of John Doe. You'll live the life of John Doe, work the job of John Doe and your body will die the death of John Doe. A wave that knows it's the ocean keeps rolling towards the shore; John Doe knowing his *Spiritual Self* keeps being John Doe—everything is natural, everything is the same. But inside, his waves are made more of dancing, not crashing. So are our own.

While the rest of the world is caught in a web of drama, we flow more and more freely. While others wrestle over what was and what might be, we are falling more deeply in tune with what is. While society thinks that this or that will bring an end to unhappiness, we know if happiness can't be found here, it isn't tied to the deeper 'I' and it won't last for long.

So on the outside, you remain what you've always been. But on the inside, the place from which you see is drastically upended. Your eyes are increasingly open. Your mind, increasingly awake. Awake from the stories of being an American, a Middle Eastern, a European. Awake from the story of being an atheist, a theist, a believer, a non-believer. Because upon waking up, it's not so straight forward—even for the religious. You wake up, you're no longer a Buddhist; you're the Buddha. You're no longer just a follower of Krishna; you're one with Krishna. You're no longer a Christian; the resurrection of Christ is within you. You see that the awareness that looks out from your body is the same awareness that looks out from your spouses. You see that the awareness that is aware of a Muslim mind is the same awareness that is aware of a Christian mind. You see that all is oneness and ease and that even though others know not what they do, that there is love at the heart of rocks and hurricanes, centipedes and the hearts of man.

It's this understanding that ushers in a new earth. When we're moving, speaking, living and relating from home, we're felt as a home for all people. As we grow in familiarity with our own deepest *being*, we start being a mirror for the deepest *being* of others. As they project their opinions and stories and dramas, they're met with no projection back, no shoulds or shouldn'ts, no reactions and belief systems, no judgements or biases. Only an open space of acceptance, of aware presence. And as they peer into our spaciousness, those who are willing fall into their own. As they sit with our stillness, those who are ready find theirs also. This makes possible a great healing for the world. Simply by being our *Self*, by mirroring, we give a great service. We make possible the healing of our mothers. We become a mirror, we make possible the healing of our children. We rest in the *Spiritual Self*, we make possible the healing of all things

This is the way to global healing, global peace. It dawns through *Self*-recognition. Through the untamed vision that, in the end, it's only 'I' in everyone. This vision doesn't come through voting booths or governments, communities or crowds. Peace on earth doesn't dawn through paychecks or belief systems. Money creates imbalance. What's in your wallet will never be the same as what's in my wallet. Belief creates opposition. Your mental position will never be everyone's mental position. The harder we identify with the outlines of our nation, the name of our social movement and the beliefs passing through our heads, the harder time we have seeing the truth, the truth that there exists but one peace, both for the individual and the world. It's the one foundation upon which experience stands. It's that which is universally shared in equal amounts within all beings at all times and is awakened through the direct recognition of our shared existence. It comes from each individual knowing that when they say 'I', that while it may refer to the body, to the mind, that it's also pointing to something a little more inward than the body, a little bit deeper than the mind, a little bit more universal. And in being universal, it's a little more true. It's less our thinking, more our being. It's less our body, more the *deeper 'I'* expressing itself within all things.

The start of this new world is in each of us. No effort to spark it is in vain. Nothing we do to raise human energy is wasted. No shift of attention away from the old mind, the separate mind and towards unity, acceptance, wholeness and love is lost. It's all adding up. It's all serving to usher the human family out of the rain of individualism and under the roof of the soul.

It starts today with us. It starts each moment of our choosing. Each moment we choose to be poured out of our dramas. Each moment we choose our likeness found in others and see it's 'I' behind their eyes. Each breath we choose *presence* over preference, *awareness* over judgement, *love* over fear. In all these instances, we aren't just taking steps in our own journey. We aren't just welcoming the *light of life* more deeply into our lives. We're turning on the *light* for the whole human family, for our children and their children and their children and theirs—we're preparing the way that brings the whole world home.

DIRECTLY HOME

7 Q&A'S

QUESTIONS ON MEDITATION
AND SPIRITUAL PRACTICES

'You seem to say we should disregard the mind entirely. But isn't this just a form of avoidance and spiritual bypassing? What about handling personal traumas and deeply rooted attachments?'

It's one thing to release surface-level thoughts and conditionings; another to release the more deeply held ones.

Imagine you're pouring out a coffee cup. The coffee inside the cup has been sitting for two weeks. What's resting at the top is easy to pour out. But what sits at the bottom—what's been the most deeply carried and held to—is a different story. It's thick and congealed. You may have to go into it a little more. You may have to dig into it, because it won't just pour out like the rest.

It's the same with us. There are times of deeper work. There are subconscious blocks and stagnant energy that need exploring and excavating before we can fully self-empty. I highly recommend investing in a therapist or life coach for these. But meditation can help here as well. Because meditation isn't just a tool for discovering our depth of *being*. Meditation is also a path for recognizing the hang ups and roadblocks that keep our hearts from living there.

So when to give traumas and attachments our attention? When you have a particular mental loop you keep falling into—explore that loop. When you find a part of the world you can't seem to surrender—look at that part. Become very curious and interested. Be very aware of the energy of it. Why is it there? How does it feel? What thoughts and sensations accompany it? The more clearly we see these, the more easily we can free ourselves. It's like shining a flashlight in the dark—naturally seeing it makes it easier to approach.

So be courageous. Sit with the traumas. Explore the thoughts that keep sticking in your mind. Then when they are released, rest another deeper layer down into your *Self*. Another deeper ideal, deeper attachment or loss or desire is bound to arise. Just repeat the process lovingly, courageously.

. . . .

'Posture gets a lot of attention when it comes to meditation. I don't hear you mention it. Does posture not matter in these practices?'

There are different ways for a batter to prepare to hit a baseball. But they all have the same aim—hit the ball.

Meditation is no different. Posture is somewhat up to the person.

So for most practices, a meditation teacher shouldn't spend too much time on posture. The role of posture is important to the degree that it allows your body to slip out of your awareness—but you remain alert, the light remains on. These conditions depend on individual bodies and minds. There is no one-size-fits-all. I recommend simply cross-legged and relaxed. I recommend this mostly because that's where my body and mind have been conditioned to 'turn off', to be at ease, to go into meditation. It's a more traditional posture and yes, there's a reason for it. It has the two qualities we're looking for: alertness and ease. But sit how it works for you. Sit how you feel alert and at ease. Meditation is meant to be carried out the front door anyway.

. . . .

'Meditation just doesn't work for me! I can't ever seem to silence my mind. Is there any hope for me?'

There's a Hindu parable. Once, a young man was unable to make progress in meditation. He'd been trying for many years, but still couldn't silence his mind. He went to his teacher to see what could be done. The teacher asked him where his mind kept taking him—what thought did it keep running towards. The young man replied, 'My buffalo. All day long, my mind is running towards my buffalo.' So the teacher sent him home to meditate on the buffalo.

The next day, he came to visit the young man. The teacher knocked on the door and asked him to come out. After some time, the young man shouted, 'I cannot come out! My horns won't fit through the door!'

Where does your mind keep running? What frees you from all other thoughts? Use that as your meditation.

QUESTIONS ON THE 'AWAKENING' PROCESS

'Why does 'awakening' happen to some and not to others?'

The *Self* is what we are regardless of if we're aware of it or not. We have to understand that first. What's true in the light is still true in the dark. Our peaceful nature is there whether we've seen it or have yet to, have discovered it and forgotten it, are moving from it or appear to be moving out of it.

Why do some realize it and not others? It has less to do with spiritual study or years of practice and more to do with what is laid on the heart.

Imagine you're running down a shoreline to your lover. Why are you running when walking would suffice? You're not running because your lover is over there and you are here. You're not running because you're not with them. What makes you run is the deep burning desire for them, the burning need to close the gap and be with the beloved face-to-face.

Desire is the road to all things. What gets a lover to the beloved? Desire. What keeps a lover from the beloved? The lack of it.

People say, 'But I desire the beloved. I desire awakening and peace and God.'

Most people have *some* desire for these. But the desire is not stronger than the desire for what sits in the spaces in between. And no one can teach us the higher desire. We can read books and go to churches and meditate and pray. But authors and preachers and Bibles can only teach you what to think about. They cannot teach you the burning desire necessary to transcend the level of consciousness from which you're currently operating. Only you do that—only *life* does that.

That's why it's important to be honest and to grow in inner honesty. Only through honesty do you see your other desires, your worldly desires are higher on your heart's wish list. Only through honesty do you see how they fail you, how they rarely meet expectations and when they do they rarely stay for long. If this level of honesty and clarity is there, the desire for the timeless grows on its own. All the suffering of life is driving us there. But it's only ever desire that draws us nearer.

· · · ·

'I know the ego is an illusion—that it's not really me. Still, it's always dragging me down in life and in meditation. I've tried the methods in this book, but I can't seem to see through it. If you could offer one bit of advice, what would it be?'

An illusion has its reality in its consistency. You see a mirage on the horizon—a green oasis. What's the first thing you do to test if it's real? You blink. You close your eyes. You empty the oasis from your mind and look again. And if it's truly unreal, after clearing it from the mind—it'll be gone.

It's the same with the ego—the consistency must be broken.

Imagine you are walking through a field—open and vast. And in the middle of the field is a yellow string. The string is as long as the field. As far back as you look, the string is there. And as far forward as you walk, the string is there. The yellow string seems to be very real, very important—it's with the field wherever it goes. But if you grab a pair of scissors and cut the string, instantly it's seen through.

Right now, you have a continuous string of thought running. It seems like you because it's always there. How to see through it? You must break the string of continuity. You must create gaps in the consistency. Each time you create a gap, it's unraveling and the natural state is becoming clearer. With devotion to this practice, clarity arises.

QUESTIONS ON SILENCE AND AWARENESS

'Silence doesn't seem to reveal much of anything to me. If I sit for twenty seconds or twenty minutes, it doesn't matter. I wind up getting more dull and lifeless than before.'

If you step out of a dark closet and into the day, what will be revealed? Not much at first. All that's been known is the dark. The eyes can't see yet, they're not adjusted. As far as they're concerned, there's nothing in the daylight. It takes a moment for things to come into clarity. So it takes patience, it takes a heart willing to sit and allow the light to settle.

You say, 'If I sit in silence, I wind up getting more dull and lifeless than before.'

Okay, why are you going into silence trying to *get* at all? Going into silence trying to 'get' is what's keeping you from it. It's like going into the world trying to acquire happiness. The harder you *try* to get happiness, the more you push it away. The trying keeps it from you. Happiness starts when you stop trying. Happiness starts when the pursuit ends. It's the same with meditation and silence. Don't go in looking to get anything whatsoever. Go in looking to *understand;* to understand things as they are, to understand you as you are, to understand life as it is. When you step out of the closet and into the sun, you aren't instantly looking to fill your hands. You're simply looking to see. It's this seeing and understanding that leads to peace—not trying to get something better. Because what you get will always leave you. What you understand is always there.

So don't go searching for bliss or 'enlightenment' or some otherworldly experience—don't go searching to get. Search for understanding. Be patient and let what *is* tell you what it is. When we stop looking to get and simply look to understand, peace comes about more and more. This doesn't mean we never get caught up in the dramas again. It doesn't mean there aren't seasons where peace feels more difficult to touch. But these will simply be opportunities for *deeper* understanding.

. . . .

'After reading your book, I'm seeing how increasing awareness makes things clearer. For the first time, I see issues I didn't even know were there. But this is also creating new problems! For instance, I've become aware of how much I tend to over-talk. Now I have trouble speaking and being present at all. This is one example, but I feel that increased awareness keeps creating new problems like this!'

Perfect. Beautiful. First, see again that awareness in and of itself is good. Awareness of self, awareness of speech, awareness of actions and awareness of others. It's good to see these. And the awareness itself is pure—it's simply awareness.

You say, 'Awareness is creating new problems!'

Is it awareness that's creating problems? Or what you're doing with awareness?

If we clean a mirror and don't like what we see, is the mirror to blame? The mirror is simply showing us what is there. The mirror is helpful. Awareness is just a mirror.

So imagine you're looking in the mirror and you don't like what you see. Perfect. You'd like to clean up. Okay. Beautiful. There are only two ways to clean up; seriously or non-seriously. This cleaning up is life or death—or this cleaning up is simply playful, simply relaxed.

Let's apply this approach to what you're seeing —'I tend to over-talk and dominate the conversations.' This reality nor the awareness are the *real* issue. The seriousness is the issue. Can you see this? A child on a playground is prone to falling. He cannot put one foot in front of the other. By all accounts, he's a bad walker. But is the child troubled? No! The child is playful. The child has awareness that he needs improving—he should learn to walk better! But he's not troubled, he keeps walking playfully. And when he falls, he falls playfully also. It's no big deal.

Let this be the case in you. Be playfully aware. See the state of things openly, non-seriously. Observe your state, your uniquenesses, your individuality and if you'd like to address things, address them from a state of play as well.

. . . .

'I can't get past the fact that being in a state of no mind feels like a step backwards. It also feels non-practical. Don't we need the mind to make it through the day? Isn't it useful?'

A hammer is useful. But if you go around hammering everything all day and night, you'll end up breaking more things than you fix.

This is what the mind is doing to the human family. It's always hammering, always being used and it creates more damage than repairs.

You say, 'Being in a state of no mind feels like a step backwards. It feels non-practical.'

If you truly explore the state of no-mind, you see it's the opposite; being in a perpetual state of 'mind' is the step backwards. When you're doing the dishes, look and see; are you thinking about the dishes? When you're driving down the highway, look and see; are you thinking about driving down the highway? When we're watchful, we see more often than not, the mind is simply stirring up misery. Perhaps that misery is a sadness over the past or fear over the future. Perhaps it's simply a subtle boredom and disengagement with life here-now. Whatever it is, it breaks more than it fixes.

This is why no-mind is a step forward. This isn't to say we *never* think. When creative thought or productive thought is needed, it rises out of our depths. It rises out of silence, which is the source from which thinking stirs. When thought rises out of silence, it's able to make more efficient use of itself. It has more energy, flow and one-pointedness. It can direct itself effortlessly towards the solution or activity of its choosing. Before, the mind was often running in circles, in a maze. Never really getting anywhere new or moving towards anything intentional, just wandering. With more and more silence, we start thinking in straight lines. We think one step at a time. In this way, thinking less raises our consciousness.

. . . .

'Being selfless and loving sound like great ideals, but they aren't practical. In fact, the more I put others first, the more I get walked over. The more I unconditionally care for others, the more they take advantage of me. Are you saying we should just be okay with this?'

The love I share is not a state of action—it's a state of being. Action is surface level. It's black or white. It's there or not. And when love remains only an action, it gets taken advantage of. If my love is dependent upon how I act, then when I act in self-defense, I act unlovingly. This puts me in between a rock and a hard place; if I remain loving, I get walked over; if I defend myself, I lose love. This is an unloving place to be.

When love is a state of *being,* love is primary; pure, actionless love, independent of circumstance. From this state, the right action comes on its own. Whatever the act may be. If our actions are giving and generous, it is the fruit of love. If our actions are defending, standing against or raising our voices, it is the fruit of love also. In both cases—giving or opposing—we are acting for the same reason; love. Love for our deepest Self, love for our shared *being.*

If someone threatens us now, we are free to love no matter the action. If someone threatens us or takes advantage of us, we are fully aware and stand up for ourselves just as we would stand up for another. We do so with no hesitation. We are fierce and uncompromising in our actions. And when the situation is resolved, we put it down. We move on and return to open awareness, which then blooms back into loving action. Yet, the whole while, whether loving action appears to be taking place or not, loving *being* remains.

. . . .

'I've listened to a lot of Self-inquiry lectures and read a lot of books on the topic. I know I am awareness, but I still don't have the peace that's said to come with it.'

We have to be honest with ourselves—do we know awareness? Or do we know about awareness?

A person may have read a lot about parachuting. Their library may be filled with manuals and how to's. But their library isn't filled with parachuting. It's filled with words. When they reach 10,000 feet, throw open the hatch and look down, they'll be faced with a wholly different reality.

You say, 'I know I'm awareness, but still don't have peace.'

Peace isn't something we come to have—it's something we realize. It's a dimension we bring into the light. It doesn't get realized through reading. Reading and listening to lectures is helpful. But don't gorge yourself on them. The real nourishment is your meditation, your practice. Teachings are only there to clarify insights from your practice, insights you're already scratching at. If not, they only confuse you. This is why there' a famous Buddhist parable on this.

Once, a Zen master turned to his student, 'How many of the Buddha's words are the devil's words?' The student replied, 'They're all the devil's words!'

'They're all the devil's words'—they're all just thoughts, ideas. Believe them and they deceive you. True spirituality takes you beyond the mind. In fact, that's what buddha means—*buddhi*; beyond intellect, beyond mind. That's the place of peace.

So be honest and faithful. Begin devoting at least three-fourths of the time you spend reading and listening to practicing inner silence, *feeling* for inner silence. With honesty and faith, the dimension of peace eventually shows up.

QUESTIONS ON TRADITIONAL SPIRITUALITY

'This approach seems to say that the more we focus on ourselves the more selfless and loving we become. But doesn't this focus on 'me' shut me off from everyone else?'

Yes. But turning away from others is the first step on the path to love. Because have you noticed this? When you're happy, you give happiness to everyone. When you're peaceful, you give peace to everyone. When you're filled with love and laughter, you give so much love and laughter to the world.

If you're already each of these, then don't turn away. It isn't needed. But if you could use more, if these aren't your inner qualities, your deepest backgrounds, what would be more impactful for you and others but to find them? And you can only discover by looking inward. It's the maturation process. A child must focus on himself before he can provide for a family. A seed must focus on its growth before it can pollinate the world. All awakened beings do the same. Whether it was Christ's forty day fast in the desert, the Buddha's forty-nine-day meditation or Muhammad's retreats to the cave of Hira. All awakened beings turned from society, responsibility, family and the world to find their inner blossoming. It's the intended progression. It's the first step before the second.

. . . .

You say several times to be one-pointed on practicing silence and meditation. Other times, it sounds like you say there's nothing we can do at all. In fact, that by trying, we get further away. Which is it?'

Planting seeds is up to the farmer and shining light is up to the sun. If the sun shines but no seed is planted, nothing takes root. If the seed is planted but no sun shines, you get the same result.

Spiritual realization is similar. We show up and do our part. We 'pick up our cross daily'. We work the inner ground and plant the seeds and do everything to create conditions suitable for spiritual flowering. And God and life meets us there.

So it's work—it's up to us. And it's grace—it's up to God. But when the process is purified, they flow together. Works dissolve into grace. This is why Christian monk Meister Eckhart says, 'If God wants to act in the soul, He Himself is the place in which He acts.' Because what is all the spiritual practice moving us towards? What do we earn by meditating and praying? What do we improve? In reality, nothing. It would be truer to say the work was to *stop* working. The work was to sit within the *source,* trust the *source,* surrender to the *source* so that what we aren't moves aside.

This is why this book and all religious paths can be summed up in one short mantra: 'Be still; know God.'

. . . .

'This spiritual approach seems very different from Christianity and western religion. I can't see how my faith could be reconciled with this. What would you say?'

Religions are like maps. They show the way that an individual walked from the physical to the spiritual. They aren't given to be argued over. They're given in hopes that those of similar mind might follow and arrive also. It's true that the details of the maps differ. They're marked by different symbols and point in different directions. But they're all means of getting to the same destination.

Compare two spiritual maps; the map of devotion and the map of Self-knowledge. One is Christianity, the other, Buddhism. They appear in opposition. One is pointing upward and the other inward. But to follow either is to arrive under the same roof—the roof of gentleness, selflessness, compassion and love. And all religions say they are simply the religion of love, that if you have faith and knowledge and belief but not love that you have nothing.

So the paths are many, but the destination is one. We can see this in nature. All plants reach for the same light. Watch a jasmine growing up a fence or a grape vine ascending its post. If you don't know the light, you'd think they're after different things. They're taking many unique twists and turns. Sometimes they appear to be going the wrong direction. Yet, it's all their own way of worshipping the one light.

The human family isn't apart from nature—we have different paths to the light. The paths aren't meant to create arguments. Arguments are for beginners. Beginners argue, spiritual kindergarteners argue. And they worship their arguments. They house dusty libraries of cumbersome books filled with them—arguments on theology, doctrine and dogma. They fill their hearts with these arguments and preach that this is a movement towards God.

Drop this. God is beyond arguments. Go to Him. Fix your eye on the *light*. Find the path that's calling to you, not the one that's calling the vines to the left or the right—but to *you,* to the individual.

A religious mind may say, 'Yes, but Jesus said he was 'The way, the truth, the life.' That 'No one gets to God but through Him.' But who is this 'me' that Jesus is referring to? Is it the body of Jesus? The mind of Jesus? Is it those parts of Jesus that are changing, that don't enter the river twice? Or is Jesus referring to the *I AM?* Is He referring to the *Absolute*; the one, timeless life and the one formless spirit?

We each must see for ourselves. That's the invitation of this book. It's mostly the path of *Self*-knowledge. But there's nothing wrong with the path of devotion. If it's yours, I celebrate you. I celebrate you and simply invite you to be devoted—*truly* devoted. Be devoted so entirely to God that you forget you're there. And in forgetting you're there, you find moments of Him living and breathing and looking out from the eyes you call your own. Then this question of different religions and paths will be there less and less.

. . . .

'You mention prayer. What role does prayer play in meditation and awakening? Do you pray?'

To me, there's only one prayer: 'God, replace me with You.' Which means either 'Return that within me which is resisting your will back into alignment with your will' or 'Use me as a creator to create what is most pleasing for You.' Both are the same prayer—both are asking for the creator essence to flow through us, for God to flow through us.

Of course, these don't have to be the direct words. The words and prayer can be more specific; 'Help me to be more like You in my relationship with my husband.' 'Help me to love like You in the workplace.' 'Help me and the world to have the acceptance of your will and what is or for your power and will to flow through me.' All of these are different prayers from the same heart. A heart asking to be more aligned with God. A heart that's working to shift all energies towards the Absolute. The more pure and continual the prayer, the greater the likelihood.

Many of us aren't ready for this prayer. There's nothing wrong with that. It's why other prayers are given. But frequently, other prayers aren't prayers—they aren't a means of surrendering and loving God—they're attempts at influencing God. They're the ego begging God for this or that, not surrendering deeper into Him.

So 'God, replace me with You.' This is the highest prayer. The mind and mouth may be saying whatever, but it's this prayer that's on the lips of the heart. The more it becomes primary in our minds, the more *God* enters our awareness. And the more God enters our awareness, the less we feel a distance between us and Him. A lack of distance between us and God, us and the universe, is far more valuable than anything else we could pray for. Jesus calls it 'The Kingdom of God'. It's the discovery that the ultimate reality of what I am and the ultimate reality of the universe are the same. To see this is not simply a one-time happening—it's a moment-by-moment thing. So the prayer doesn't stop at 'amen'. It's a living prayer. You do it without ceasing.

QUESTIONS ON ANXIETY, LIFE'S DEMANDS AND LONELINESS

'Is it your experience that thoughts of anxiety continue no matter what? I feel like sometimes teachers say that after 'awakening', such thoughts aren't there. Yes, no or we cannot know?'

Is it possible to have an 'awakening' and never 'fall asleep' again? Sure. Is it possible to have an 'awakening' and still have illusion and suffering? Sure. It depends on the individual. Just because a man loves his wife doesn't mean it's forever at the forefront of his mind. Just because we know our deepest *Self* doesn't mean we eternally live, breath and move knowingly from *Self*-abidance. So thoughts and anxieties can certainly continue. They have for me.

Imagine you're riding a bicycle. You realize you'd like to stop. But just because you lift your feet doesn't mean you instantly stop. Your momentum carries you. It's natural.

It's the same with an 'enlightened' experience. The old thoughts and feelings keep going. The difference isn't that they stop forever. The difference is that they, often gradually, get less and less of our attention. Then embodiment starts to happen. But even this can create a conflict; 'I know I'm not these thoughts and yet I keep buying into them.'

In reality, the one that says, 'I'm not these thoughts' and the one that keeps buying into them are the same. It's a subtle way of mind energy shape-shifting. It's the ego running up to the next floor, hiding behind a higher identity, a spiritual identity.

We must simply remain aware and watchful. In time, the thoughts are seen through—mind energy as a whole is seen through. We recognize that it's just the mind that's flip-flopping. It's just the mind that goes through states where it knows the *deeper 'I'* and where it gets fooled by the old momentum. All the while, we never cease being that *deeper 'I'*. The part of us that is 'enlightened' is *always* enlightened.

This can take time. It can take the stream emptying itself into the depths—mind repeatedly dissolving into its source—before that source starts guiding all its movements. This process is far from complete in me. But the less we get involved in the movements the less they show up. Naturally, you stop giving something your attention, it eventually falls outside of your awareness, then comes around less and less.

. . . .

'Every time I step towards a deeper embodiment of my Self, something comes up; a problem at work, an illness in the family, a medical issue. I've experienced this for years. Is there something at work that actually wants to keep us from awakening or is it just my mind?'

Life keeps handing us reasons to suffer as long as we're living from a place that isn't true—which is a place that isn't lasting. This suffering isn't there to trick us. It's there to guide us back.

You say, 'Every time I step towards my deepest Self, something comes up.'

Beautiful. These things aren't obstacles. They're the way. They're teaching us how to step into our depth of *being*. They're showing us what creates anger and where we need to soften. They're showing us where we're attached to the world and how we need to let go. And they're everywhere.

Every feeling, thought and interaction is the teacher we need. Every sensation, perception and experience is the teacher we need. This doesn't mean we always like it. It doesn't mean the teacher is always friendly and non-imposing. Often, it's the opposite. It's tough love. It's in your face, uncompromisingly. But the teacher is a teacher, nonetheless.

You say, 'Is there something at work that wants to keep us from awakening?'

To me, it's the opposite; when we're on the path—when our hearts are *truly* set on love and freedom and *home*—everything in existence is working in our favor.

. . . .

'My journey into spirituality has been the greatest joy of my life. Still, I often feel somewhat lonely. Few share in the joys I've found and I have less and less in common with those around me, including many relationships I've had my whole life.'

If a hundred seeds fall on rocky ground and only one longs to be a flower, she's going to have to go alone. And in going alone, she'll feel quite lonely. She won't burst into bloom overnight. She'll spend some time in the darkness, some time on rocky ground. But she's following a natural longing; the longing for life, for her fullest potential, for her inner truth.

It's the same for spiritual seekers. Before we 'come to full bloom', we often feel a void over the connections and relationships we've lost. It's a sacrifice all seekers make. To awaken to our spiritual *Self,* we stop identifying with the old mind. The mind of separateness, judgement and reactivity. The framework of society is built on these. We see it in the news, in politics and entertainment. And when we truly look into the nature of our relationships, we find the same. Many of them revolve around identities of brokenness, blind judgments and taking issues with life. As we begin feeling more whole and accepting, this way of relating becomes more foreign. We find our minds are less and less in accordance with other minds. If our mind is not in accordance with other minds, naturally we can feel a bit like an outsider.

You say, 'I have less and less in common with others.'

Beautiful. This is good. It shows you're dropping the commonality you had between yours and other's minds so that you might step closer to your commonality with *life*. It shows you're dropping your opinions that this is better than that, that 'there' is greater than 'here', that 'us' is better than 'them' so that you might draw nearer to the source within all things. And besides, you're in good company. No one ever found God by pretending to be like everyone else. There are a growing number of seekers doing just this. There are a growing number of seeds who've left the rocky ground, but have yet to come to full bloom.

Some teachers will say the loneliness felt here is ego. It must be observed and transcended. But the desire for relationship is good. It's a natural desire. It's the desire for sharing, connection and love. These are the desires of the *soul.* Listen to and embrace them. Don't lose yourself in thinking the spiritual life is a life of isolation. To me, that life is one of limitation. It says that spirituality can only exist outside of relationship, outside and away from the world. This is a great misunderstanding. The true spiritual life is the normal life. It's right where we are. And that life includes relationships and flat tires and taking out the trash and chatty neighbors.

Don't deny loneliness. Listen to your longing. Find a community. Forge relationships with those who are on the journey. Perhaps they'll be far ahead of you. Perhaps far behind. But if they're on the path, that's all that's needed for fulfilling, spiritual relationship. And these are the relationships that add value to your life and your spiritual walk. In the meantime, don't turn others away. Be the light. If you truly start blooming, those who haven't will notice. And the more fully you blossom, the more you'll be inviting them to join you. May this help move our hearts and minds towards the deeper truth for them also.

WORD FROM THE AUTHOR

Hello friend,

Thank you for reading *Directly Home*. I pray the words within these pages helped in some small way. If they did, shoot me a message/email and let me know! If they didn't, shoot me a message/email and let me know!

Either way, a short cautioning and invitation: the methods and approaches in this book are not meant to be used as an excuse to ignore, avoid or check out from the 'real world'—something I've seen far too often when it comes to the meditative path. The methods, approaches and *reality* pointed to in this book are meant to be integrated *into* your 'real world' life.

To me, that's the key to whether spirituality becomes a source of great health or another obstacle along the way—integration. If you awake tomorrow to find you've won the lottery and start pretending the life you had the day before never happened, you're bound to stir up trouble. Your new wealth is meant to be integrated into your existing roles, responsibilities and relationships.

So it is with understanding our spiritual wealth. Things will naturally get adjusted here and there, but we aren't meant to throw out the old and shut ourselves away or uproot the foundation of our lives. We're meant to integrate the spiritual into the ordinary; the grand into all the simple day-to-day roles life asks of us.

If you're struggling with this integration process, looking for further spiritual clarity or need help to begin embodying the message of this book, there are plenty of online resources and communities ready to serve. Choose mine (visit me at my website: exhalenow.co) or choose someone else's. But get involved.

The road *home* is shorter when taken together.

In service,

Barrett Self
barrett@exhalenow.co
exhalenow.co

ABOUT AUTHOR

Barrett Self invented cheesecake, the wheel and those little scratch-and-sniff stickers that everyone forgot existed but always enjoyed at the time. He's climbed several mountains—tall ones. He's led several dangerous expeditions—the kinds no one else would do. Once, while on a hike through the Appalachian jungle, he successfully hypnotized a group of gorillas into thinking they were Barrett Self. Today, they're living in peace and harmony, driving electric cars and manufacturing those little scratch-and-sniff stickers that everyone forgot existed but enjoyed at the time.

For anything that Barrett has actually done or that might be useful, you can follow him on the socials or find him on his website, exhalenow.co

Printed in Great Britain
by Amazon

84744917R00108